The 2016 election was certainly filled with its daily share of surprises. Hillary Clinton ran the most expensive campaign in history and despite the cards being stacked in her favor, the polls showing her winning by a landslide and a strong assumption amongst many that her election was already a given, she lost and lost big. The shockwaves amongst her followers are still in full motion. How could she have failed so massively. Her new book *"What Happened"* reflects the shock. However, unless you were living in a bubble, a coma or just not paying attention you should know what happened. *Everybody Knows What Happened Except Hillary Rodham Clinton.*

Clinton was living in a liberal, elitist, bubble of self-entitlement. Her arrogance and smugness were apparent to everyone outside of her bubble. She could not connect with the common people including her core base which were flocking to Bernie Sanders; an obscure 75-year-old Senator and self-proclaimed socialist. Despite the dirty tricks of the Democratic National Committee (DNC) and Clinton herself, she never regained the allegiance of her core base.

She entered the race with much baggage. Scandals follow the Clinton's and while none have stuck to them, yet, the sheer volume of scandals and mysterious deaths associated with those scandals is enough to raise eyebrows of anyone but her diehard supporters.

She surrounded herself with people who told her only what they thought she wanted to hear. Either they were inside her bubble or simply did not want to upset her and face her oft reported temper. Many of the people in her inner circle also became subjects of various scandals during the campaign as well. The media fed her delusion as well. Their hatred for the Republican candidate skewed their reporting in her favor through both stories and polls. In doing so the media seriously damaged their credibility for many years yet to come. They also prevented Clinton from glimpsing outside her bubble.

She took no responsibility for her actions or claimed responsibility but turned around and blamed others. In her mind, she could do no wrong. She is responsible for everything having to do with her e-mail scandal. She chose to use a private server, store it in her home and wipe the drive clean. She is responsible for claiming to turn over all pertinent e-mails when in fact she did not. She is the one who put national security at risk. Her husband's secret tarmac meeting with Attorney General Lynch only lead to further speculation that a cover-up was in motion. FBI Director Comey's censuring Clinton's carelessness in protecting secret information, her claims of not knowing what was classified and her release from charges that so many of our military folks would have been locked up for only fueled the notion that powerful people were protecting her criminal acts once more.

During the election, the DNC computers were hacked and e-mails were released to the public. Clinton and the DNC began pointing fingers in every direction. They insisted that the culprits be found, but did all they could to obstruct a formal investigation. They feigned fury but were building a smoke screen to distract people from the damning contents of those e-mails which denigrated their loyal followers and showed a clear link to the DNC causing harm to the Sander's campaign. Their eventual finger pointing would be at Russia. They had no evidence but claimed Russia colluded with Trump. As much as Clinton and the DNC claimed to want to find the underlying cause of the hacking, they would not allow the FBI access to the computers. It has since become known that the hacking was an internal job. The false allegations have caused our relationship with Russia to implode.

Clinton decided to play the women's card, even producing actual cards with the word woman on them. Her record on women's rights was far worse than Bernie Sanders. She stated a woman who claims rape should be believed, but history has shown that her husband's accusers were not given that respect and it has been claimed Hillary Clinton herself threatened those women if they spoke out. She chose to include her husband in the campaign and not surprisingly, both of their records on women were exposed.

Clinton focused on celebrity fundraisers in New York and Los Angeles but despite the influence of celebrities, it was the people in middle America that felt ignored and who in the end decided the election. Clinton made some attempts to appear as a regular person during the campaign. She seemed scripted and fake. Her efforts backfired. The Clintons may be less wealthy than the Trump's but they are still wealthy. Harry Truman once said, "You can't get rich in politics unless you're a crook." Choosing to wear a $12,000 jacket while discussing income inequality was a poor choice. Claiming her family was dead broke after leaving the White House should and did raise a lot of questions about how they became wealthy, with many suspecting they sold government access and influence.

In questioning how the Clinton's become wealthy, they claimed it was due to book deals and paid speeches.

The speeches received enormous fees making people question whether they were merely a sham to pay for political influence while Mrs. Clinton was Secretary of State. As more e-mails become known and the timing of speeches are compared to State Department decisions it becomes more obvious that the Clintons were selling political influence to the highest bidder.

The Clinton Foundation stood at the heart of many scandals that dogged Hillary Clinton's failed 2016 presidential campaign. Donations to her family's controversial charity began to dry up soon after her November loss. Just weeks after the election, donations to the foundation from foreign governments plummeted, some as much as 87 %, while donations from the corporate sector dropped by 37 %. The Clinton's had no product left to sell.

Her inner circle was also rife with controversy and scandal. Her bizarre closeness with Huma Abedin raised many questions including whether their closeness extended into a secret love affair. Whether true or not, Abedin was constantly at Clinton's side and doting on the candidate creating an elephant in the room situation. Abedin's family and her own past clearly showed connections to Saudi Arabia and the Muslim Brotherhood. People questioned whether the Clinton campaign had a spy in their midst or secretly embraced Saudi Arabia, a country which donated enormous amounts of money to her campaign and her family's foundation. Abedin also used Clintons private e-mail server and sent confidential information to her husband Anthony Weiner's unsecured laptop. Abedin was not the only questionable character in Clinton's inner circle. Brazile, Wasserman Schultz, Podesta, Mook, Bill

Clinton, Weiner, and others brought injected baggage and additional scandals to the campaign.

Hillary Clinton lacked the excitement to engage the large crowds that both Donald Trump and Bernie Sanders attracted. She focused on small venues. It was her hope that the affection many people held for her husband, Bill Clinton could help her raise the excitement level. Bill Clinton, like Hillary Clinton are both polarizing and have just as many people who love them as hate them. Using Bill Clinton in the campaign was a calculated risk that in the end appeared to be a miscalculation and unnecessary distraction. His campaign appearances were removed.

Each of these factors, and more discussed in this book, demonstrates why *Everybody Knows What Happened, Except Hillary Rodham Clinton.*

To Run or Not to Run

Anyone with half a brain knew that Hillary Clinton had ambitions to run for president in 2016. Her thirst for power was palpable. Part of her strategy was to feign lack of interest in becoming president and pretend that she was entering the race at the behest of the masses. She wanted to appear to be a selfless savior of the left, answering a clarion call not of her making.

According to the Reuters Nov. 5, 2010 article, *In New Zealand, Mrs. Clinton told a pair of television interviewers that she won't run for president even in the aftermath of this week's congressional midterms that saw Republicans take control of the House and make big gains in the Senate. Some have suggested that Mrs. Clinton should take advantage of President Barack Obama's unpopularity to make a new bid.*

But Mrs. Clinton said that she was very happy in her role as America's top diplomat and would not be the first female president of the United States.

She told one interviewer that the United States "should be" ready to have a woman as commander in chief. Yet, when asked if that could be her, she answered: "Well not me, but it will be someone."

Asked by another interviewer if she would rule out a White House run in 2016 or before, she replied: "Oh yes, yes."

It is fully understandable that a sitting Secretary of State would not declare wanting to run against her boss, Barack Obama in 2012. She was part of his team and arguably in a role that had more power and significance than Vice President Biden. She may have desired to run against Obama in 2012 but it would not have been in her interest to do so. She would have appeared disloyal. She was, however, disingenuous in saying she would not run in 2016. All her actions were leading her to a second Presidential run.

> According to the Hill, October 18, 2012, *Mrs. Clinton elaborated on her position. Secretary of State Hillary Clinton hopes to be "cheering" for the country's first female president, but said it absolutely will not be her.*
>
> *She said, as she has on numerous occasions, that she has no desire to remain in politics following her retirement this January.*
>
> *"I hope to be around when we finally elect a woman president," she said. "That would be a great experience for me, to be up there cheering."*

Despite her denials, Mrs. Clinton had in fact been running for president and building her credentials since she rewrote the duties of her ceremonial position as First Lady to include more substantive duties such as health care reform. Once the Clinton's left the White House they had no intention to move back to Arkansas. Hillary Clinton needed to establish herself as a resident of a state that held more influence and a reliable liberal constituency. New York was her best bet to become Senator which was her next step to running for President.

After the ugliness of the 2016 campaign it's hard to remember just how ugly the 2008 democratic election was. Neither candidate felt much threat from John McCain who simply lacked any charisma or devout following. The real battle was between Clinton and Obama who were not friends by any stretch of the imagination. Their contempt for each other was evident during their campaign and debates.

On March 7, 2008 Obama's campaign manager had the following statements to CNN. *"Considering the huge amounts of money, they have made in recent years, they've contributed their money to the campaign, some of those relationships financially have been with individuals who have come under quite a bit of scrutiny for possible ethics transgressions, its essential to know where the American people are getting their money from,"* Plouffe said Thursday.

"If Sen. Clinton is not being open and honest about her tax returns or her experience on the campaign trial, you have to wonder if she'll be open and honest with the American people as president," he added.

A perception that Hillary Clinton and Bill Clinton are dishonest has followed them since their days in Little Rock. While Bill Clinton has the charm and charisma to spin a negative story into a positive light. Hillary Clinton does not have the likability nor oration skills to do the same. They are both perceived to be dishonest but Bill Clinton at least has the likability factor.

On Jun 9, 2016, the Daily Caller reflected upon comments made by Obama during the 2008 campaign. The following is dialogue from an Obama campaign advertisement.

"It's what's wrong with politics today," the narrator said. *"Hillary Clinton will say anything to*

get elected. Now she's making false attacks on Barack Obama. The Washington Post says Clinton isn't telling the truth." Attacking both Clintons' dishonesty was a theme of the Obama campaign.

In an interview with ABC News, Obama said Bill Clinton "continues to make statements that are not supported by the facts ... This has become a habit, and one of the things that we're going to have to do is to directly confront Bill Clinton when he's making statements that are not factually accurate."

Clinton in turn did her fair share of smearing her opponent. On February 25, 2017, the Huffington Post also reflected upon the 2008 democratic primary.

"Throughout the 2008 election season, racist and bigoted smears about Barack Obama circulated online, and bubbled up into mainstream conversation about the campaign in the traditional news media. Two of the most prominent lies about Obama, which persist to this day, were that he is secretly a Muslim (playing on fear-mongering and bigotry about Islam), and that he was not really born in America. Both of these ideas paint Obama as "other" and outside the mainstream, drawing their potency from fears about Black people gaining power. People generally associate these memes with the right wing. But the truth is that for the entire Democratic primary, not only did Hillary Clinton's campaign do nothing to push back against the racist fear-mongering about Obama, it actually fed this atmosphere and helped it grow. It was a part of their strategy from early in the campaign."

After her failed 2008 democratic presidential candidate bid, she brokered a deal with Obama to become his Secretary of State, a position that would give her access to foreign policy and which holds more power than the mostly symbolic Vice President position. In exchange, she pledged her support to Obama and worked to sway her voters to support him as well. Despite their hatred for each other after a bitter campaign, somehow, they managed to merge into what the public accepted as a unified team. Politics.

The conflict was address in New York Magazine News and Politics on November 21, 2008.

> *"Obama and Clinton might be headed: toward a kind of reconciliation that eluded them even after the hatchets were supposedly buried and their nomination fight was over.*
>
> *No one disputes that the implications of this putative development are huge: for Obama and the Clintons, for foreign and domestic affairs. And opinions differ wildly over whether the pairing would be a stroke of genius or a match made in hell. But what strikes me as most interesting about it—along with the other appointments Obama has made so far—is what it suggests about the President-elect, from his conception of his embryonic administration to the size and contours of his ego.*
>
> *The sheer improbability of the thing is striking, too, of course. All the happy-pappy posturing of the general election—the emphatic endorsements, the labored "unity" in Denver, the energetic stumping by Hillary for Barack, the two-way tongue bath between*

42 and the soon-to-be 44 at a rally in Florida in the campaign's final week—did little to alleviate the bedrock enmity between the two sides. The Clintons continued to regard Obama as a featherweight, a phony, a usurper. Obama neither liked nor trusted nor thought he needed Hill or Bill; he bridled at their apparent insistence that he kiss their rings."

They did need each other though. Obama needed Clinton to sway her voters his way and to do so as smoothly as possible. He also needed to ensure she would not challenge him in 2012. Hillary Clinton needed a consolation prize that would further her goal of securing the Presidency in 2016.

Given that Barack Obama did not fully endorse Clinton in 2016 until after the democratic primaries had concluded suggests his support was more gratuitous than heartfelt. This impacted her 2016 run for President.

According to the Washington Times, May 23, 2016 report quoting esteemed journalist Carl Bernstein the impact was evident.

"Carl Bernstein, who wrote a biography on Mrs. Clinton, told CNN this campaign season that Mrs. Clinton has a "difficult relationship with the truth" and has become a "specialist" in fudging facts."

What happened: Dishonesty.

Hillary Rodham Clinton and her followers love to tout her being the most qualified candidate to ever run for president. She certainly held several prestigious positions that should lend credibility to these claims, at least if she was moderately successful in these positions.

Clinton is certainly intelligent. Her undergraduate class chose her to be the first student speaker ever to present a commencement address. Her comments on the Vietnam war made national news. Her graduate studies at Yale also demonstrated her academic abilities. She is remembered by some for her poise and negotiating skills as she led sometimes volatile discussions on controversial issues of the day. She was still a first-year student but leading groups of mainly 2nd and 3rd year, male students, one of which was to become her future husband, Bill Clinton.

To be such a successful student, she needed to have a good memory for details. As a law student, she has been trained in how to treat sensitive information and how to read documents for proper dissemination. It is therefore somewhat mind-boggling that she would later defend her not understanding that a "C" on state department documents meant confidential. The e-mail scandal will be discussed in a later chapter, but for now just keep in mind she is intelligent. Intelligence does not negate a moral deficiency.

When Bill Clinton became the Governor of Arkansas, Hillary Clinton became the new First Lady. This role is usually ceremonial with the First Lady choosing a few projects close to her heart to champion. Hillary Clinton chose education. In 1977, Hillary co-founded and drew up the articles of incorporation for the Arkansas Advocates for Children and Families, a group that for nearly four decades since has fought for expanded opportunities in early education, juvenile justice reform, increases in state funding for child health care and other major initiatives.

Apparently, she did not find a conflict of interest in representing an accused child rapist who even she concedes she thought was guilty. According to the Steam,

> "Mrs. Clinton staged a successful defense of 41-year-old Thomas Alfred Taylor, an Arkansas man accused of the rape of a 12-year-old girl.

> Mrs Clinton later discussed the case candidly on an audio recording first uncovered by the Washington Free Beacon's Alana Goodman, telling a journalist named Roy Reed that she harbored little doubt as to his guilt. Still, she helped Taylor duck a harsh sentence.

> "Oh, he plea bargained," she told Roy with a brief spout of laughter. "Got him off with time served in the county jail, he'd been in the county jail about two months."

One could argue that as a lawyer, she had no choice in who she represented, but that is not the case. She was not a public defender. Her specialty was finance law. She took this high-profile case for exposure and notoriety. Her selfish need to advance her career went entirely against the mission of the Arkansas Advocates for Children and Families. She did get noticed though, by the Rose Law Firm.

Hillary Clinton was quickly approached to join the Rose Law Firm. At the time Bill Clinton was the Attorney General of Arkansas. She became the first female associate and quickly became the firms first female partner.

The Daily Signal clearly explained Clinton's experience at the Rose Law Firm on March 13, 2015.

"Clinton always seems to be present when critical documents aren't. One needs to look no further than her involvement with the Rose Law Firm more than 20 years ago, which provides valuable insight into the woman who once again finds herself under fire for similar allegations.

Most Americans have forgotten, but in the 1990s, Hillary Clinton gained notoriety by being the first First Lady in American history to be called to testify in front of a grand jury. Not only was Hillary called to testify, but as part of the grand jury investigation, she became the subject of accusations of suspicious activity concerning missing subpoenaed records from the Rose Law Firm where she had worked in the mid-1980s. Of interest to prosecutors were records from the Whitewater land deal in Arkansas and Hillary's legal representation of convicted felon Jim McDougal's savings and loan association, Madison Guaranty.

The Rose Law Firm records involved a particular phone call and transaction involving Hillary that was "intended to deceive financial regulators," according to a Frontline series by the Public Broadcasting Service. Federal bank regulators went so far as to call the financial deal involving Hillary and the Rose Law Firm "a sham."

But for Hillary, a sitting first lady, the subterfuge was only beginning. Federal prosecutors subpoenaed documents surrounding the real estate transaction, but the papers went missing for two years—until January 1996—when Hillary's aide reported that they had magically appeared in the book room on the third floor of the White House in the Clintons' personal residence.

With no explanation provided by Hillary regarding the subpoenaed documents, which turned out to have been in her custody the entire time, investigators called in the Federal Bureau of Investigation to "ascertain [Hillary's] role in their mysterious disappearance." An FBI fingerprint analysis of the Rose Law Firm billing records revealed there were two significant sets of fingerprints on the missing subpoenaed documents—those of White House Deputy Legal Counsel Vince Foster and Hillary Clinton.

The Senate Whitewater Committee, which at the time also was investigating the matter, ultimately concluded the documents indeed had been placed into the book room by Hillary Clinton herself. Hillary of course stated she had "no idea" how the documents had ended up there.

In the midst of the investigation, Foster died in what was ruled a self-inflicted gunshot wound, and more chicanery surfaced—a hard drive from Foster's White House computer went missing. It eventually turned up in the Old Executive Office Building across the street from the White House, but investigators ultimately were unable to recover documents from the hard drive because it had been significantly damaged."

The Rose Law firm started out as a prestigious post for a newly graduated law student and rising to partnership so quickly was both an acknowledgement of Hillary Clinton's academic success as well as her influence over her husband, the Attorney General of Arkansas.

Due to her influence over the Attorney General and soon Governor of Arkansas Hillary Clinton helped the Rose Law Firm triple profits. Hillary Clinton's employment at Rose Law firm should have been a highlight of her early career, but as the 2008 election approached, she no longer had any mention of the Rose Law Firm on her websites. The Rose Law Firm website also had no mention of Clinton having worked there, even though she was their most famous employee. Mrs. Clintons next accomplishment was serving as the First Lady of the United States.

First Lady is a ceremonial title that is bestowed on the spouse of the President and is not an elected position. Their duties are largely ceremonial. Mrs. Clinton enlarged her role more than any other First Lady including her husband famously proclaim that she was Co-President. She was not. Her ambitions dictated that she develops a purpose beyond the traditional role. She moved the First Lady's office from the East Wing to the West Wing, nestled amongst the President's advisors. She was determined to remain visible. She became an unofficial adviser to the President.

Her most important assignment was to help create universal healthcare thus fulfilling one of her husband's campaign promises. By all accounts she worked very hard at creating what was later dubbed "Hillarycare". Unfortunately, her penchant for secrecy became problematic.

The New York Times, December 5, 1993 reported on a lawsuit against Clinton and the Health committee for lack of transparency.

"A Federal district judge considered (sic) the legality of Hillary Rodham Clinton's influential role in formulating health policy for the nation.

In a lawsuit filed (sic), two groups of doctors and health policy advocates invoked a 1972 law, the Federal Advisory Committee Act, to insist that meetings of the President's Task Force on National Health Care Reform be "open to the public."

The law generally requires Federal advisory committees to conduct their business in open meetings. But it makes an exception for "any committee which is composed wholly of full-time officers or employees of the Federal Government." The plaintiffs contend that Mrs. Clinton's group does not qualify for an exemption because she holds no job in the Government.

"The regime of openness in government has been built by a lot of people sympathetic to Hillary Clinton," said one plaintiff, Peter T. Flaherty, who is president of the National Legal and Policy Center. "Now she would just sweep away those statutes because they're inconvenient to her."

17

Throughout the 2016 campaign Clinton was haunted by the repetition of her secrecy and a perception that she was not trustworthy and did not believe that the same rules others had to abide applied to her. When she sought input from senior members of her own team, she was only looking for agreement and any advice that did not match her opinion, no matter how minor was batted away. She cursed out one advisor who told her that the plan was too grand and would never make it through a congressional vote. When she approached respected members of congress, democrat and republican, she was greeted warmly. Everyone seemed to want her to succeed. She politely listened to their advice even when told that the plan was too grand, would not pass a congressional vote and would be rejected by the American public. She was advised to break the plan into smaller changes to be implemented over time. To her folly she ignored the advice and kept her plan intact. The plan was rejected by congress without ever being brought up for a vote.

Her first venture into the political world was a failure but it was also an opportunity for her to learn the political dance which she would soon become a master at when she became Senator.

In 1999, Hillary Clinton formed an exploratory committee to pursue the possibility of running for the U.S. Senate seat in New York. The seat was resigned by long-time New York Senator, Daniel Patrick Moynihan. In February 2000, the First Lady officially launched her senate campaign with an announcement at the State University of New York. She was elected with 55% of the vote.

Hillary Clinton's senate career had been touted in many speeches as an example of why she was best suited to become president in 2016. After all, U.S. Senator is a very prestigious title. She had all the connections to be highly successful and the support and experience of her husband to guide her. There are reasons why those who touted her senate career never mentioned any specific accomplishments.

According to the National review, July 28, 2016, *"Hillary's senate career is defined by safe, noncontroversial bills, most of which were essentially pure fluff and yet she couldn't get them passed. In her eight years in the Senate, just one of Hillary's bills got enacted into law. This bill designated the U.S. courthouse at 40 Centre Street in New York City as the "Thurgood Marshall United States Courthouse."*

Hillary had eleven other bills that were passed by the senate but none of them made it through the house. Four of those bills were to rename U.S. Postal Service offices. Then there was another courthouse renaming, a commemoration of the 75th anniversary of the Military Order of the Purple Heart, and another commemoration for the 225th Anniversary of the American Revolution.

There only seems to be one explanation. Hillary already knew that the Democrats would eventually nominate her to be President. Her strategy was thus to do nothing while Senator that could possibly be used against her. The amazing thing is that she couldn't even get these pieces of fluff passed. At the end of the day, her legislation didn't really do much to help everyday Americans."

As already mentioned, the 2008 democratic primary was brought out the worst in Barack Obama and Hillary Clinton. They really had a hatred for each other that remained after the mudslinging had stopped. Despite Clinton having no foreign policy experience, Obama touted her as the best person suited to take charge of our foreign policy as Secretary of State. As the adage goes, keep your friends close and your enemies' closer. In offering the position to Clinton, Obama would have the only person who could undo the negative campaign on his team. He needed her voters to win. He also knew if her constituents were not pacified he may need to face Clinton in a 2012 run off.

According to Forbes, June 10, 2014, *"Diane Sawyer asked Hillary Clinton a question that should've come as no surprise: What significant things did she accomplish during her four years as Secretary of State? What's surprising is that Hillary didn't even attempt to answer the question."*

According to the New Republic, June 9, 2014, *"Clinton's critics, such as Charles Krauthammer, say she accomplished little of note in the job, and has no major accomplishments to her name. According to her admirers, Clinton was a successful secretary of state who did much to enhance America's reputation in the world. Her critics are correct in the sense that her record isn't particularly impressive.*

If you want to get a sense of how puny Clinton's accomplishments at State were, you should read not her haters but her admirers. On Sunday in The New York Times, Nicholas Kristof devoted a whole column

*to praising Clinton's record, and yet was unable to
list anything that wasn't a broad generalization."*

The truth was her tenure as Secretary of State was
mediocre at best. Lacking excitement, Clinton tried to
embellish her heroism by claiming she landed in Bosnia
under gun fire and needed to scurry for protection. Videos
of the event show her walking leisurely to a tea ceremony
set up on the tarmac.

There is broad, general talk of how Clinton helped
to restore and rebuild how America is perceived abroad.
She certainly did travel more than any other Secretary of
State.

According to the New Republic, June 9, 2014,
*"Even if she had some relative successes in these
areas, America's global popularity has declined since
she took the job."*

Even if we remove the e-mail scandal and its broad
impact on National Security, the travesty of Benghazi, and
the ongoing investigation into influence buying by foreign
interests through the State Department, exorbitant speaking
fees for Bill Clinton and massive foreign donations to the
Clinton Foundation during her tenure; her ranking as
Secretary of State could be considered mediocre at best.
Factor in the scandals and her tenure can be best described
as disastrous and self-serving.

Her accolades are most impressive if we base them
simply on job titles. Her accomplishments in each were far
more limited. She branded herself as a champion for
children based upon writing the charter for Arkansas
Advocates for Children and Families but the importance of
that role is diminished by her seeking fame through

representing a man that even she felt was a child rapist in a high-profile case to gain attention for herself. Her partnership in the esteemed Rose Law Firm should garner her credit, if it were not for the scandal that followed and her direct obstruction of the investigation through hiding documents. Her senate career should be a crowning jewel on her career but instead of accomplishing anything of significance or being bold and brazen, she saw this position as merely a stepping stone and played it safe, leaving with only one accomplishment, renaming a federal building.

She was never prepared to be President, she merely prepared the illusion that she was the most prepared. This is the past but it is the foundation on which she chose to run and it did impact her 2016 run for President.

What happened: Baggage.

Mrs. Clinton has been reported by insiders as having a violent temper and being merciless on people who disagree with her or stand in her way. The people who she allows to join her inner circle know this, and while they are true supporters of hers, they would likely be very reluctant to express any opinion they knew she would not agree with. It would be easy to dismiss one or two comments as simply the venting of disgruntled workers, but the sheer volume and consistency of these reports lend credibility to the reports. The notoriety of some of the people reporting fortifies the contention that Mrs. Clinton's temperament and persona are indeed a subject of concern.

On May 23, 2016, the Washington Times reported on Mrs. Clinton's temper. *"In an exchange detailed by Ronald Kessler, who wrote "First Family Detail," a look at the Secret Service and the families they guard, a member of the uniformed Secret Service once greeted Mrs. Clinton, "Good morning, ma'am," to which she replied: "F– off."*

"When in public, Hillary smiles and acts graciously," Mr. Kessler wrote. "As soon as the cameras are gone, her angry personality, nastiness, and imperiousness become evident. ... Hillary Clinton can make Richard Nixon look like Mahatma Gandhi."

David Brooks, a columnist at the New York Times, wrote last year: "In normal times, [Mrs. Clinton] comes across as a warm, thoughtful, pragmatic and highly intelligent person. But she has been extremely quick to go into battle mode. When she is in that mode, the descriptions from people who know her are pretty much the same, crisis after crisis: hunkered down, steely, scornful and secretive."

In one incident, Mrs. Clinton berated a low-level campaign worker for making a scheduling mistake, the Post reports, and when the girl turned her back on Mrs. Clinton to walk away, Mrs. Clinton grabbed her arm.

"Bill Clinton and Hillary's campaign team are concerned that her anger may surface at the wrong time," the Post reported. "They are concerned that she could have a serious meltdown in front of TV cameras, which would make her look so out of control that voters would decide she doesn't have the temperament to be commander in chief."

On November 26, 2014, MSNBC had a similar assessment. *"Both Clintons' temper emerged as a theme in several interviews, but Hillary Clinton's "had much more sustained velocity, for a longer period of time," according to former White House Chief of Staff Leon Panetta. "She just let everybody have it," Panetta recalled of one incident.*

In another incident, he recalled an aide telling him: "The First Lady just tore everybody a new asshole."

Joan Baggett, who served as assistant to the president for political affairs, said people didn't feel comfortable pushing back on the first lady, even when she was wrong.

"She would blow up over something that she misinterpreted. Again, you can't take her on, that's

not my boss. You can't take on the First Lady,"
Baggert said. "I remember one time in one of these
meetings where she was blowing up about [Bill
Clinton's] staff and how we were all incompetent and
he was having to be the mechanic and drive the car
and do everything, that we weren't capable of
anything."

Baggert added that Clinton would chew out staffers
in front of their colleagues, which made things
especially awkward. "Sometimes she'd be in those
meetings and I'd think, 'Please don't let her yell at
me,' Baggert added."

Joan Baggert's assessment was correct and directly
relevant during Clinton's failed Presidential bid in 2016. To
reside in Clinton's inner circle bubble, a person needed to
conform to her opinions. She was surrounded by yes men
and women. Nobody wanted to give her negative news or
news that would suggest she was wrong about anything. If
Clinton declared an object to be blue, it was blue, even if it
was really red. Without any means of checks and balances
she became more delusional in her convictions. Her
delusion and disconnect was fortified by her team's
unwillingness to provide her with a reality check.

On October 1, 2015, the National Review had an
even more scathing assessment of Hillary Clinton's
temperament.

"Hillary was very rude to agents, and she didn't
appear to like law enforcement or the military,"
former Secret Service agent Lloyd Bulman recalls.
"She wouldn't go over and meet military people or
police officers, as most protectees do. She was just

really rude to almost everybody. She'd act like she didn't want you around, like you were beneath her." "Hillary didn't like the military aides wearing their uniforms around the White House," one former agent remembers. "She asked if they would wear business suits instead. The uniform's a sign of pride, and they're proud to wear their uniform. I know that the military was actually really offended by it." Former agent Jeff Crane says, "Hillary would cuss at Secret Service drivers for going over bumps." Another former member of her detail recollects, "Hillary never talked to us. Most all members of first families would talk to us and smile. She never did that."

Within the White House, Hillary had a "standing rule that no one spoke to her when she was going from one location to another," says former FBI agent Coy Copeland. "In fact, anyone who would see her coming would just step into the first available office." One former Secret Service agent states, "If Hillary was walking down a hall, you were supposed to hide behind drapes used as partitions." Hillary one day ran into a White House electrician who was changing a light bulb in the upstairs family quarters. She screamed at him, because she had demanded that all repairs be performed while the Clintons were outside the Executive Mansion.

*While running for U.S. Senate, Hillary stopped at a 4-H club in upstate New York. As one Secret Service agent says, Hillary saw farmers and cows and then erupted. "She turned to a staffer and said, 'What the f*** did we come here for? There's no money here."*

Secret Service "agents consider being assigned to her detail a form of punishment," Kessler concludes. "In fact, agents say being on Hillary Clinton's detail is the worst duty assignment in the Secret Service."

What Happened: Temperament

Benghazi, it does make a difference

The public did get a glimpse of Clinton's personality transformation during the Benghazi hearings. As Secretary of State, Clinton had a duty to protect Americans abroad and in particular American diplomats. She was brought before this congressional committee to ascertain if she was negligent in fulfilling this role as it pertained to Benghazi.

After several hours of questioning Clinton lost her composure and went on the attack. Her body language, voice, facial expressions, and tone all changed. Anyone who was watching the hearings noticed. The words she spoke became a rallying cry for continued transparency on the Benghazi attack and haunt her through the 2016 election and beyond.

> *As reported by ABC News, October 22, 2015, "With all due respect, the fact is, we had four dead Americans! Was it because of a protest or was it because of guys out for a walk one night and decided they'd go kill some Americans?! What difference, at this point, does it make?!"* Americans were dead and their deaths may have been prevented if she had not been negligent of duties.

On September 11, 2012, the US consulate and CIA annex were attacked in Benghazi Libya. The attack resulted in the deaths of Ambassador Stevens, Information Officer Sean Smith, and two CIA operatives, Glen Doherty and Tyrone Woods. A terrorist act is often sudden and without warning. In this case, there were more than enough warning signs that the situation in Benghazi was not stable.

In April 2012, two former security guards for the consulate threw an IED over the consulate fence; the incident did not cause any casualties. Just four days later, a similar bomb was thrown at a four-vehicle convoy carrying the United Nations Special Envoy to Libya, exploding close the UN envoy's vehicle without injuring anyone. In May 2012, the International Red Cross office in Benghazi was attacked. Al-Qaeda claimed responsibility for the Red Cross attack. The Red Cross suspended operations stating they were extremely concerned about the escalating violence in Libya.

The same Al-Qaeda linked group released a video of what it said was its detonation of an explosive device outside the gates of the U.S. consulate on June 6, which caused no casualties but blew a hole in the consulate's perimeter wall. The group left behind leaflets promising more attacks against the U.S..

British ambassador to Libya Dominic Asquith survived an assassination attempt in Benghazi on June 10. Two British protection officers were injured in the attack when a rocket-propelled grenade hit their convoy. The British withdrew all consular staff from Benghazi in late June

On June 18, 2012, the Tunisian consulate in Benghazi was attacked by individuals affiliated with Ansar al-Sharia.

According to a local security official, he and a battalion commander had met with U.S. diplomats three days before the attack and warned the Americans about deteriorating security in the area. The official told CNN that he advised the diplomats, "The situation is frightening; it scares us.

Ambassador Stevens' diary, which was later found at the compound, recorded his concern about the growing al-Qaeda presence in the area and his worry about being on an al-Qaeda hit list. Additional security was requested for the mission in Benghazi but was denied by Charlene Lamb at the U.S. State Department. They were desiring to project an image of normalcy.

Clinton initially took the responsibility for the failure to provide additional security but subsequently back-tracked. She now claimed "The specific security requests pertaining to Benghazi ... were handled by the security professionals in the [State] Department. I didn't see those requests, I didn't approve them, I didn't deny them."

Clinton, Obama, and many government officials tried to cover up the fact that this was a terrorist attack and touted a story that the attack was a spontaneous reaction to an obscure YouTube video titled the Innocence of Muslims. The maker of the obscure video was arrested by federal officials despite there being no connection between his video and the attack. He remained held on separate charges that he violated his probation by using a pseudonym in making the film. After a great deal of pressure, Clinton, Obama, and other government officials changed their story and labeled Benghazi as a terrorist attack and unrelated to the YouTube video.

It's important to note that as the event was occurring in Benghazi, Clinton sent a message to her daughter Chelsea, via the unsecured server, and stated that a terrorist attack was currently occurring in Benghazi.

There was no mention of a spontaneous protest nor a connection the YouTube video. Spectators on the ground also confirmed that there were not protests prior to the terrorist attack on the consulate.

It's hard to decide if the actual attack or the attempt to cover it up was more detrimental to the victims and their families. The families need closure and they were denied it. The families wanted the truth and tried to get it from Clinton.

> According to the Conservative Tribune, December 10, 2015, *"Democrat presidential candidate and former Secretary of State Hillary Clinton mercilessly threw the families of Benghazi victims Chris Stevens, Sean Smith, Glen Doherty and Tyrone Woods under the bus on Sunday in a bid to divert blame away from her own despicable subversion of the truth.*
>
> *"I can't help it if the people think there has to be something else," Clinton replied when ABC News host George Stephanopoulos asked her why she misled the victims' families by blaming the 2012 Benghazi attack on an Internet trailer of an anti-Islamic movie.*
>
> *She went on to cite the "fog of war" for causing a mix-up of information, then claimed that she did not discover the actual truth — that the attack occurred as part of a terrorist plot — by the next morning."*

Hillary Clinton's e-mail to her daughter Chelsea shows she knew this was a terrorist attack. She was lying to the families of the victims.

The Conservative Tribune continues, *"Yet the House Select Committee on Benghazi revealed two months ago that Clinton knew within hours of the attack that it had been planned by radical Islamists and did not occur spontaneously in response to some video.*

Moreover, when Clinton met with the victims' family members at Andrews Air Force Base two weeks after the attack occurred, she still continued to peddle a false narrative about a horrible video that made all the Muslims in Libya mad.

"I gave Hillary a hug and shook her hand, and she said, 'We are going to have the filmmaker arrested who was responsible for the death of your son,'" Charles Woods, father of deceased CIA contractor Tyrone Woods, told Fox News in late October."

The cover up may or may not be of Clinton's making. It appears that Obama may have played a greater role. All the video footage covering the attack was retrieved and should have been able to provide some answers but it was deemed top secret and locked away even from members of congress involved in the investigation.

The reason additional security was not provided, why military planes were not sent in and why the story has been covered up is currently speculation. Evidence suggests that the CIA annex was being used to smuggle weapons to "moderate" forces in Libya and that many of those weapons ended up on the hands of Al Qaeda. If this is true it is very likely that the weapons used in the attack were American. If the videos were released the weapons might be identified as American and jeopardize the covert CIA mission.

There is also evidence that weapons deals were made through the Qatari government to supply "moderates" in Syria wishing to overthrow Assad. Those "moderates" morphed into the group now known as ISIS. This is what the Russians have also contended and would also explain the almost instantaneous rise of this new, major terrorist group. Turkey and Russia have separately accused the United States of backing what they call "terrorist groups" in Syria. Turkish President Erdogan said that he had evidence that US-led coalition forces give support to ISIS.

The investigation concluded with few questions answered. Many of the needed documents were never provided to the committee.

According to Newmax, December 12, 2016, committee member *"Pompeo criticized the report for not faulting former Secretary of State Hillary Clinton, and released a supplement, along with Rep. Jim Jordan, concluding that Clinton "failed to lead" as the head of the State Department, and that the administration "misled the public" about the attack in Benghazi."*

It is important to note that newly discovered Clinton E-mails which she did not turned over to the FBI are related to conversations about Benghazi.

What Happened: Deceit

Inside the bubble

Hillary Clinton surrounded herself with people who thought as she did. There were rarely dissenting voices to be heard and certainly never twice. This is what life in a bubble means. Everyone believes, thinks, and says the same thing. Most American's do not live in a bubble. We talk to each other, we debate, we disagree, we agree or come to an understanding. Sometimes our mind will be changed by a well-articulated opinion from someone else. We grow as individuals.

Mrs. Clinton had every reason to believe that she was winning and would win the election. She had every reason to believe that she was connecting with the voters and that she was much adored. She had every reason to believe that she was invincible. She had every reason to believe these things because she lived in a bubble and only associated with people she allowed in her bubble. If nobody would tell her otherwise she could only assume all was well.

Dictators surround themselves with people who agree with them. They are robbed of the ability to hear opposing opinions and often feel invincible. Saddam Hussein had an inner circle that never questioned his actions and only told him what he wanted to hear. He was confident that the American's would back down and never actually invade Iraq. His inner circle fortified this belief right up until the American's began their "shock and awe" bombing campaign on Bagdad. Effective leaders require people who are willing to express opposing view, even if it is only in private.

According to Forbes February 28, 2012, *"Our inner circle is a critical instrument in our leadership toolkit. We need to take a hard look and consider whether we are inviting only "safe" people into that circle at the detriment of our organizations and ourselves.*

Sometimes the most loyal colleagues are the ones who are courageous and caring enough to tell it to us straight; to tell us when we've stepped in it; to advise that a mid-course correction may be necessary. And, yes, to tell us when we've done a good job.

When it comes to the workplace and our role as leaders, it's our responsibility to maintain a balanced perspective and stay attuned to the truth about our words and actions, the impact we have on others, and the perceptions we create. The leader is isolated from reality, surrounded by a small group of people who deliver the good news and hide the bad. The leader's entire worldview is distorted, controlled by those who are feeding his or her perceptions.

Often the leader rewards the peddlers of feel-good information and punishes the purveyors of truth. In either case, it's a dangerous position for any leader.

Part of being an authentic, effective leader is recognizing that we have blind spots, and then seeking – and accepting – critical feedback from trusted advisors to ensure we maintain a balanced perspective."

Even before she was First Lady it was noted that Mrs. Clinton did not like or appreciate people disagreeing with her on even minor issues. She has a clear pattern of rewarding those who agree and punishing those who dissent.

She approached voters without knowing that she was perceived as cold, untrustworthy, elitist, self-serving and unlikable. She kept to small venues while Bernie Sanders tended to the masses. She held lavish fundraisers while mostly ignoring the actual voters. When she switched tactics, it seemed fake. Above all she did not comprehend that the voters were looking for a candidate who was not part of the establishment and she embodied the establishment.

Clinton's most recent scandals were certainly on the voter's minds. Her dismissive attitude in calling her e-mail scandal a "nothing burger" or callously saying "what difference does it make", at the Benghazi hearing showed a lack of understanding that these issues were indeed important to voters. She received advice from several of her inner circle that she should joke more about the e-mail scandal. This was poor advice.

What Happened: Disconnect

Feeling the Bern

Bernie Sanders was an unexpected phenomenon during the democratic primary. A little-known senator from Vermont who was elected as an independent and proclaimed himself a socialist was rallying massive support from people on the left who viewed Clinton as an establishment candidate. Clinton failed to change her platform to match the desires of much of grassroot democrats. She also failed to see the discontent of many voters and the power of Sanders to rally them.

Martin O'Malley and Bernie Sanders were not meant to win. The DNC did not choose them to win prior to the primaries. They knew they wanted Clinton. Sanders and O'Malley were meant to be window dressing highlighting the democratic party as being diverse but still unified. Sanders was likely surprised himself by his popularity, especially amongst young voters.

In the beginning, the media paid almost exclusive attention to Hillary Clinton. As time progressed though, and Bernie Sanders was attracting huge crowds of enthusiastic voters. Some rallies were estimated to be 100,000 people. Clinton on the other hand was speaking at small intimate events, often with handpicked attendees. The news began giving more airtime to covering Sanders. The Clinton campaign had to finally notice.

On May 23, 2016 Washington Times reported *"This fall, when her poll numbers were slipping in the race against Vermont Sen. Bernard Sanders, the New York Post reported: "Hillary is furious — and while Clinton advisers think that may save her, it's making the lives of those who work for her hell."*

"Hillary's been having screaming, childlike tantrums that have left staff members in tears and unable to work," a campaign aide told the Post. "She thought the nomination was hers for the asking, but her mounting problems have been getting to her and she's become shrill and, at times, even violent."

Despite being in politics for 34 years, Sanders was viewed as an outsider during a time when people were questioning the establishment. This is perhaps due to his earning his senate seat as an independent, or perhaps because he was a self-proclaimed socialist. He did not have the baggage that Clinton was weighed down with. He had not been a part of any major scandal. He was charismatic and likeable. What Hillary lacked, Sanders had.

He tried to keep his campaign free from negative politics. While the country was focused on Hillary's e-mail and Benghazi scandals he did not feel the need to pile fodder on these issues. He focused instead on character issues.

Clinton tried to portray herself as a civil rights candidate. Her husband had a decent record of accomplishment on civil rights issues which she tried to absorb as her own. She did not have a large portfolio herself, and that which she had was often more symbolic in nature.

According to The Washington Post, February 25, 2016, a protester cornered Clinton during a small fundraiser confronting Clinton with the candidates own past comments. "They are often the kinds of kids that are called 'super-predators,' " Clinton said in 1996, at the height of anxiety during her husband's

38

administration about high rates of crime and violence. "No conscience, no empathy, we can talk about why they ended up that way, but first we have to bring them to heel." Clinton is wrapping herself in the flag of Obama to appeal to Black voters, arguing that she's the candidate who will address the needs of Black people. She's got her surrogates attacking her opponent's civil rights bonafides, and she's built a large stable of Black establishment players to support her. Clinton is proclaiming that Black Lives Matter and offering bold promises to fight systemic racism and inequality.

The Huffington Post, February 25, 2016 reflects back on Clinton's comments during the 2008 campaign and how she repackaged her message for 2016.

"But it's hard to believe she's serious about fighting for racial justice unless you pretend her 2008 campaign against Obama never happened. If you remember that period, there's good reason to believe today's promises are nothing more than lip-service to a community she sees as key to winning the nomination.

Clinton is now attacking Bernie Sanders for having criticized Obama, trying to take advantage of Black folks' desire to defend the president. But it was Clinton herself who waged an incredibly nasty campaign of attacks and smears against Obama, going far beyond mere policy disagreements. A quick trip down memory lane reveals that Clinton has a history of employing race in a divisive, cynical manner.

39

Based on what happened the last time Hillary Clinton ran for President, we should expect that at some point Black people will get thrown under the bus again, especially if it helps Clinton gain or maintain power.

Painting Obama As Not 'Fundamentally American'

Throughout the 2008 election season, racist and bigoted smears about Barack Obama circulated online, and bubbled up into mainstream conversation about the campaign in the traditional news media. Two of the most prominent lies about Obama, which persist to this day, were that he is secretly a Muslim (playing on fear-mongering and bigotry about Islam), and that he was not really born in America. Both of these ideas paint Obama as "other" and outside the mainstream, drawing their potency from fears about Black people gaining power. People generally associate these memes with the right wing. But the truth is that for the entire Democratic primary, not only did Hillary Clinton's campaign do nothing to push back against the racist fear-mongering about Obama, it actually fed this atmosphere and helped it grow. It was a part of their strategy from early in the campaign."

On June 11, 2016, Downtrend highlighted the hypocrisy that is Hillary Clinton by reminding her of some of her publicly made racists comments. *"If the media wants to focus on the racism of the presidential candidates, why are they ignoring these 10 prime examples:*

In 1974, after Bill Clinton lost his bid for a Senate seat, Hillary lashed out at campaign manager Paul Fray calling him a, "f*cking Jew bastard!" This outburst was witnessed and confirmed by 3 people.

While serving in the US Senate, Hillary tried to make a joke that disparaged a civil rights icon and demeaned all people from India. "I love this quote. It's from Mahatma Gandhi. He ran a gas station down in St. Louis for a couple of years. Mr. Gandhi, do you still go to the gas station?" asked Clinton.

In 2005 Hillary said, "I am adamantly against illegal immigrants." She also, as a Senator, voted to construct a wall between the US and Mexico. Considering the main "proof" of Trump's racism is that he opposes illegal immigration and wants to build a wall, isn't it odd that Hillary gets off for having said the same thing?

During the 2008 democratic primaries Hillary Clinton's campaign started the "birther" rumors, questioning Obama's US citizenship. They even circulated the now famous picture of Obama in full Muslim garb. Somehow Trump's campaign to get Obama to release his birth certificate is racist, but Hillary's role in starting the birther movement is not.

Also during the 2008 presidential race, Hillary's husband Bill said this of Obama: "A few years ago, this guy would have been getting us coffee." Hillary didn't say this one but her husband did and she certainly never disavowed it.

In November of 2015, Hillary called people in this country illegally "illegal aliens." Trump is a racist when he says "illegal aliens," why isn't Hillary?

In April of this year, Hillary joined NYC Mayor Bill de Blasio on stage at a democratic fundraiser for a scripted joke about how lazy black people are. The two liberals made reference to "colored people's time" which is a super-racist way of saying black people are chronically tardy and lethargic.

April was a great month for Hillary's racism, as she also made a comment disparaging Native Americans. She said she had experience dealing with wild men when they "get off the reservation." In essence she said Native Americans are savages who must be segregated from the rest of society.

Hillary has a history of pandering to minority communities as does the democratic party. They cluster minority people into voting blocks, and often assume that the democrats have these voting blocks locked up. This is insulting to minority groups because people are not groups they are individuals who have a right to vote the way they choose. 2016 was particularly nasty due to more militant voices within these groups professing anyone who doesn't vote democrat is not really, black or gay or Latino.

Hillary's record on civil rights is not bold nor anything to be proud of. It is mediocre at best. Bernie Sanders on the other hand was authentic. He fought for civil rights for over 50 years, even when it was not popular for him to do so. Civil rights were not a campaign slogan for Sanders it was his passion. Hillary's record paled in comparison.

On July 22, 2015 Salon highlighted some of Sanders' accomplishments and civil rights endeavors. *"Much of the criticism of Sanders seems more rooted in who he is — an old white guy from Vermont — than what he has done. If anything, the fact that he has done so much for civil and minority rights despite the fact that his constituency is not one that would naturally demand it speaks to his character and wide empathy that isn't shared by many politicians."*

If the Clinton campaign were to be believed, one lingering blemish on Bernie Sanders' candidacy for the Democratic nomination is his indifference to racial justice and civil rights issues.

The truth is, Sanders has a 50-year history of standing up for civil and minority rights. Sanders does have a record of fighting on these issues, and it should be only natural for him to be able to comfortably address them before a diverse audience.

International solidarity was an unusual concept for any American to have in the 1950s, let alone a high school student. But one of Sanders' first campaigns was to run for class president at James Madison High School in New York City. His platform was based around raising scholarship funds for Korean war orphans. Although he lost, the person who did win the campaign decided to endorse Sanders' campaign, and scholarships were created.

As a student at the University of Chicago, Sanders was active in both the Congress on Racial Equality

(CORE) and the Student Nonviolent Coordinating Committee (SNCC). In 1962, he was arrested for protesting segregation in public schools in Chicago; the police came to call him an outside agitator, as he went around putting up flyers around the city detailing police brutality.

Marching in March On Washington: Sanders joined the mega-rally called by the leaders of the civil rights movement, a formative event of his youth.

40 years ago, Sanders started his political life by running with a radical third party in Vermont called the Liberty Union Party. As a part of the platform, he called for abolishing all laws related to discrimination against homosexuality. Sanders was a strong supporter of legislation to end workplace discrimination against LGBT Americans.

While mayor of Burlington, Vermont, Sanders formally protested the Reagan government's policy of sending arms to Central America to repress left-wing movements. In 1985, he traveled to Nicaragua to condemn the war on people there.

While President Bill Clinton and most Democrats in Congress supported so-called welfare reform politics, Sanders not only voted against this policy change, but wrote eloquently against the dog whistle politics used to sell it, saying, "The crown jewel of the Republican agenda is their so-called welfare reform proposal. The bill, which combines an assault on the poor, women and children, minorities, and immigrants is the grand slam of scapegoating legislation, and appeals to the frustrations and ignorance of the American people along a wide spectrum of prejudices.

In the 1990s, there was a successful effort to end the Pell Grant program for prisoners, which was one of the most effective ways to reduce recidivism. Only a handful of members of Congress voted against the legislation, and almost all of them were members of the Black Caucus. Sanders was one of the few white members who opposed this effort.

A frequent critique of Sanders is that he is from a very white state. While this is true, he certainly has not ignored issues that matter to people of color. In 2002, he achieved a 93 percent rating from the ACLU and a 97% rating by the NAACP in 2006.

The USA PATRIOT Act was passed in a 98-2 vote in the Senate and a 357-66 vote in the House. Sanders voted against it, and has voted against renewing it every single time. The law has been used to violate the rights of Arab and Muslim Americans, but few know how extensively it has been used in the drug war; from 2009 to 2010, the law was invoked for 3,034 narcotics cases and only 37 terrorism cases.

Sanders was opposed to U.S. involvement in both Iraq wars. While many simply talked about the war in terms of the impact it would have on the United States, Sanders went further, saying that the "death and destruction caused" would "not be forgotten by the poor people of the Third World.

In 2014, young immigration activists repeatedly tried to talk to Democratic frontrunner Hillary Clinton to ask her about executive action. While Clinton did not talk to them, Bernie Sanders was not only willing to talk, but agreed with their call for executive action.

Hillary Clinton may have talked about a desire to help minority populations, but Sanders had a history of action and advocacy. Hispanic voters were flocking to Sanders.

The Clinton team came up with an ill-conceived strategy to reach Hispanic voters. They launched the 7 things Hillary has in common with your Abuela (Grandmother). The role of Abuela in the Hispanic community comes with much respect, earned through strength, consistency, and compassion. It is not a role that anyone can simply inject themselves into, especially a flawed candidate such as Hillary Clinton.

Social media was merciless in responding. Comments such as, "Not my Abuela", "7 things Hillary has in common with the devil", "my grandmother is not a criminal" and "bruja (witch) no abuela" inundated the internet. Her attempts to connect seemed like mere pandering. The strategy and any reference to it were quickly disposed of.

Clinton also had an advantage in claiming the title of being the woman's candidate; after all she was a woman. She tried to monopolize on her gender by even issuing a physical woman's card as part of her campaign. She raised 2.4 million dollars "giving away" this card to donors.

According to the Washington Times, February 23, 2015, *"During her time as senator of New York, Hillary Rodham Clinton paid her female staffers 72 cents for every dollar she paid men. From 2002 to 2008, the median annual salary for Mrs. Clinton's* *female staffers was $15,708.38 less than what was paid to men, the report said. In 2006, they earned 65 cents for each dollar men earned, and in 2008, they earned only 63 cents on the dollar. Mrs. Clinton has spoken against wage inequality in the past. In April, she ironically tweeted that "20 years ago, women made 72 cents on the dollar to men. Today it's still just 7? cents. More work to do."*

According to CNN, October, 21, 2016, *the Clinton Foundation's gender wage difference was worse. "Hillary Clinton says men and women should make equal pay. But the Clinton Foundation's leadership team had un average $81,000 average gender pay gap, according to the most recent figures available.*

This pay gap was so wide that the Clinton campaign worried that the "huge discrepancies" would be noticed by journalists, according to internal Clinton campaign emails exposed by WikiLeaks."

Clinton ran on a campaign of being a woman's advocate and a need to ensure equal pay. In both instances where she could actually ensure equal pay for women, she did not. Most people will never witness the gender/pay discrepancy because it does not appear until a person is earning over 100,000 per year and is only really apparent once the 250,000 per year mark is reached. This is not of concern to most American's.

Clinton was criticized for taking large donations from countries such as Saudi Arabia (20 million) that do not afford basic rights to women or homosexuals. Even in the campaign she did not walk the walk.

The Sanders campaign focused on being a grassroots movement and professed its reliance on small donations. Clinton went after big donors aggressively which included CEO's, Celebrities, Wall Street bankers, Foreign donors and special interest groups. Given the then, and now allegations that Clinton engaged in money for access while at the State Department these large donations were suggestive that she would be paying back favors to nefarious groups if she were to be elected President.

What Happened: Hypocrisy

The Friends We Keep

The people we surround ourselves with reflects who we are. They either help us rise to new heights or pull us down with them. Hillary surrounded herself with people who contributed to pulling her down. Some came with baggage, others with skeletons in their past. Others however had more contemporary scandals directly related to the 2016 campaign. A few were just creepy.

Bill Clinton:

Bill Clinton and Hillary Clinton go hand in hand. Bill Clinton has been very influential in Hillary Clintons rise starting with her partnership at the Rose Law Firm. Her position was essential in the rapid increase in size and revenues of the firm in large part because she could influence the Attorney General of Arkansas and later the Governor of Arkansas. The inside advantage was priceless. He brought her to the White House as First Lady, and afforded her opportunities to head committees that had never been afforded to other First Lady's.

He was still popular during Hillary's senate run, at least amongst democrats. Moving to the liberal and influential state of New York helped ensure his influence would help her win her senate seat. At the time, the effects of his China policies were not apparent, The housing market crash which was caused by his kickbacks to bankers who loaned to people who were not deemed qualified had not yet caused the housing market crash, foundation questions had yet to be raised and his extra-marital affairs seemed to be more limited and forgiven by most. He was certainly a positive force in the senatorial campaign.

The 2016 campaign was a very different story. The first issue was that Hillary needed to shed the image that her successes were all due to riding her husband's coattails, which in fact they were. She needed to project herself as a strong, independent woman worthy of the presidency based upon her own merits. It is for this reason that he was not involved in the early stages of the campaign.

His absence was noted. Speculation began that the couple's marriage had dissolved or was a marriage of convenience. The unusually close and inexplicable relationship between Hillary Clinton and Huma Abedin renewed the speculation that Hillary was a lesbian, and once again that her marriage to Bill Clinton was a farce based upon political gain. They balanced each other out. His strengths were her weaknesses and vice versa. Bill had charisma, a way with words and likability. He could connect with ordinary people in a way that she could not. She needed to bring him into a more active role in the campaign.

This was a far riskier decision that it was during her senatorial run. People were now aware that Bill Clinton's China policies fleeced his pockets at the expense of creating a trade deficit with China and allowing it to develop its military capabilities using American technology. Many people understood that his economic policies involving how banks make housing loans, also known as scarecrow loans caused the housing market to crash and many people to lose their homes.

As Bill became more active in the campaign, so did his critics. Women who were accusing Bill Clinton of abuse became more vocal in their accusations and were implicating Hillary Clinton as an enabler and accused her of threatening them if they spoke out. He was greeted by posters, billboards, and people wearing t-shirts accusing him of being a rapist. The same protesters injected themselves into live camera reporting. In the best-case scenario, his presence was distracting voters from hearing Hillary Clinton's campaign messages. At worst, his presence was destroying her campaign which focused on women's issues.

In the heat of the campaign a new allegation arose that Bill Clinton had an illegitimate son via an African American prostitute while he was Attorney General of Arkansas. Danney Williams claims to be the son of Bill Clinton and that Clinton will not acknowledge him, nor provide DNA to prove or disprove the claim. It appears now that Monica Lewinsky has agreed to allow semen sample to be taken from her famous blue dress, so perhaps Mr. Williams will have his day in court after all.

Bill was Hillary's anchor, but now the anchor was tied around her neck. Exit Bill Clinton.

Chelsea Clinton:

Many of us remember Chelsea growing up in the White House and realizing how difficult that living situation must be for a child. Many of us also realized that whether we liked the adult Clinton's or not, they loved and protected Chelsea.

It was thought that Chelsea, now an adult, could be an asset in bringing Hillary's message to the younger generation which were flocking to Bernie Sanders. Intelligence must not be genetic. Chelsea has two very intelligent parents but she does not come across as very bright and at times clueless. Furthermore, reports from her co-workers suggest that she has an even nastier disposition and sense of entitlement than Hillary.

Like her mother, Chelsea is neither motivational nor inspirational in her speech. She is concise, speaking with little rambling or verbal fillers. She is very practiced. Like her mother, she has an uneasy relationship with the media. She is cautious, deliberate, disciplines and keeps an iron grip on her own narrative. Reporters threaten that control. She also controls her inner circle who must tread cautiously or risk expulsion. Her friend's responses to media questions seem very practiced and always paint her in a positive light. Their responses have at times been so similar as to sound scripted.

Chelsea's biggest contribution to the campaign came through leaked e-mails which she mentioned serious concerns about her father's closest aides trying to cash in by using his name to gain access to government officials on behalf of paying clients, aka pay for play access.

Debbie Wasserman Schultz:

Debbie Wasserman Schultz served as chair of the Democratic National Convention (DNC). She had been accused of and denied skewing the democratic primary in favor of Clinton. The entire primary is really a farce. The DNC can choose any candidate they want regardless of how people vote in the primary. Choosing someone other than who the voters choose comes with great risk of alienating and losing voters. The purpose of the primary is rally voters behind the party's candidate. Clinton was the DNC choice. They did not expect any worthy challenges and in fact they were treating the election as a coronation. Inside their bubble they could not understand that Clinton's baggage had caught up with her and voters saw her as the establishment's candidate while Sanders was considered a grassroots candidate, far more in touch with the people than Clinton.

Schultz oversaw primary debates. She angered many by scheduling few, resulting in protest from Sanders supporters who felt that more debates were warranted and would show the differences between the two candidates and likely swaying undecided voters towards Sanders. Debate rules were also adjusted so the audience was not, in theory allowed to react. In other words, it would be difficult for someone tuning into the debates to know who was winning. The Mayor of Flint supported Sanders vocally in the days approaching the debate but was told to stop or risk not being allowed to attend the debates. The debates were also very choreographed to avoid much interaction between candidates. The primary started to look like it was rigged.

The people seemed to favor Sanders and this was a problem for Clinton and her DNC backers. Together they worked to ensure the super-delegates remained steadfast behind Clinton. Super-delegates are DNC and party officials who vote independent of how people in their state vote. In New Hampshire, Sanders trounced Clinton by an historic 22-point lead, but when the 29 delegates for New Hampshire were split, Sanders was give 15 and Clinton was given 14. Most voters were dumbfounded. Some were furious. Already feeling the primary was rigged they now had what they thought was a smoking gun. The DNC claimed all was proper and super-delegates can vote as they wish. The dismissal from the DNC elite enraged Sanders voters.

Then DNC e-mails were released through wiki-leaks which showed exactly how Wasserman Schultz had in fact rigged the primary in favor of Clinton. Many Sanders supporters refused to endorse Clinton and looked towards third party, republican and write in candidates. For many it also created disillusion in the democratic primary process where they thought, erroneously, that their vote mattered.

A lawsuit filed against the DNC for rigging the election. It concluded in August 2017. The judge found those who filed did not have cause to file, but in a bold move also decided that the charges against the DNC were all valid. Rigging had occurred in the 2016 primary.

Wasserman Schultz is currently embroiled in other scandals.

Robby Mook:

Robby Mook was the young, quiet, campaign manager for Hillary Clintons campaign. He was known for his desire to work in the background and not be part of the limelight. Behind the scenes, he was a force to be reckoned with and well versed in dirty politics. He had lists of loyal supporters that he referred to as Mook's Mafia. He was able to direct actions of others so they would appear to be external from the campaign and insulate Hillary Clinton from any backlash. He directed his operatives to "smite" republicans at every possible chance. This took the form of forming groups to antagonize republican supporters, disrupt town hall meetings and take the reins of any negative stories leaked about the opposition. He was also responsible for guiding Clinton to try to confuse the public by linking the e-mail scandal and the Benghazi scandal together, creating confusion on both issues until the public grew too wary to care anymore about either. His behind the scene activities were highlighted when e-mails were released to WikiLeaks.

Huma Abedin:

Huma Abedin was never far away from Hillary Clinton, catering to all her needs. She even traveled with Clinton on the now infamous "Scooby" van tour. Their extraordinary **closeness** was hard for many to understand leading to much speculation throughout the campaign. Abedin had more than her share of baggage as well as baggage she shared with Clinton.

Abedin worked as the Deputy Chief of Staff for then Secretary of State Clinton under a "special government employee" arrangement that allowed her to serve private clients with consultant work while employed with the government. A special Government employee must work no more than 130 days in the government position per year. That does not appear to be the case for Ms. Abedin. She worked as a consultant for Teneo as well as the Clinton Foundation. Teneo is a consulting firm representing some of the largest businesses in the world. The conflict of interest in combining these multiple roles is staggering. This is part of the pay for play scandal currently surrounding, both Clinton's, Abedin, and the Clinton Foundation. Recently obtained e-mails of Abedin show this was exactly what was occurring.

Abedin also had an e-mail account on Clinton's private server and used it for government business. She likely did not consult with Hillary about which e-mails Hillary had deleted because Abedin's e-mail account had sent and received e-mails between the two that Clinton had not exposed.

Records indicate that Abedin was overpaid during her maternity leave. At the time, the government was paying her 155,000 per year. Other records showed the State Department inspector general claimed that the trusted Clinton confidant owes the government nearly $10,000 for violating rules regarding vacation and sick leave.

Abedin was born in Michigan but at age 2, her family moved to Saudi Arabia where she was raised. According to the New York Post, November 6, 2016, "Her father co-founded the Journal of Muslim Minority Affairs, and after his death in 1993, her mother, whose writings subscribe to Sharia law, took over as editor-in-chief, a post she holds to this day. The journal has published articles in favor of female genital mutilation, the sexual subjugation of women and murder of apostates. Earlier this year, The Post reported that Abedin was listed as assistant editor on the masthead from 1996 to 2008; the Clinton camp said she was only a figurehead." Her role is uncertain and her connection to the Muslim Brotherhood remains vague. It is important to note that Hillary Clinton's largest donation was 20 million dollars she received from Saudi Arabia.

Egypt has designated the Muslim Brotherhood as a terrorist group. The United States House has passed a resolution to designate them the same. Both Clinton and Obama had established connections with the group.

Abedin's real downfall was related to the scandals surrounding her now ex-husband, Anthony Weiner.

Anthony Weiner:

Anthony Weiner was a U.S. Senator and was married to Huma Abedin during the election. According to ABC News, August 30, 2016, "In May of 2011, a photo of a man in underwear appeared on Weiner's Twitter account but was later removed. After several days of swirling rumors, he claimed his account had been hacked. The scrutiny only intensified as he appeared evasive and inconsistent in public. Just days after the hacking claim, he broke down in tears as he admitted to sending inappropriate online messages to several women." The scandal at that time forced Weiner to resign from his job. Weiner apologized and was forgiven by his wife, but his internet encounters continued. On September 2016, Weiner was investigated by the FBI for sexting with a 15-year-old girl. His laptop was seized and emails related to the Hillary Clinton email controversy were found on it, causing a controversy late in the presidential election.

John Podesta:

John Podesta was the chairman for the Hillary Clinton 2016 presidential campaign. According to Judicial Watch, March 11, 2014, "The Podesta biography also includes a long history of scandal-management and cover-up for the Clintons. Podesta now says he will serve only a year as counselor to President Obama, but if the going gets tough, expect an extended tenure. Slamming House Republicans as "a cult worthy of Jonestown" is a signal that Podesta will not go quietly into the night.

Podesta played a role in managing many of the scandals that surrounded the Clintons, including Mrs. Clinton's amazing profits trading cattle futures,

Whitewater, Monica Lewinsky, impeachment, and perhaps most tellingly, the Travel Office affair. In May 1993, a senior administration official, David Watkins, fired all seven members of the White House Travel Office to make way for Arkansas cronies of the Clintons. A picaresque enterprise with lucrative connections to the airline charter business, the Travel Office handled travel arrangements for the White House press corps—it operated literally on the fly and ran its business in much the same way.

President Clinton simply could have asked for the resignations of the Travel Office employees. Instead, in actions directed in part by Mrs. Clinton, the employees were driven from office, cashiered as crooks and lowlifes. Travel Office Director Billy Dale's experience was especially harrowing: indicted on embezzlement charges, he faced up to 20 years in prison. His career in ruins, he twisted in the wind for more than two years until a jury cleared him of all charges, returning a verdict after deliberating less than two hours."

Podesta's e-mail release was blamed on a Russian hack, but as the investigation progressed, sources outside the DNC suggest that due to the transfer time of information, it was an inside job and the e-mails were likely placed on a portable device such as a flash drive. It was an internal job with a probable suspect being Seth Rich, an employee for the DNC who was murdered under suspicious circumstances in May 2017. The DNC refused to release computers and servers to the FBI for investigation.

The e-mails showed that Podesta had contact from current State Department personnel who filter information about the status of Clinton's ongoing e-mail server scandal.

The e-mails also showed Obama was not only aware that Clinton used a non-governmental computer for her work, but that Obama even contacted Clinton via her personal server despite Obama's initial denial that he knew the server existed

Regarding Hillary's private server e-mails Podesta suggested that Clinton should dump her e-mails the sooner the better. The campaign explained this as not his suggestion that she get rid of the e-mails but rather dump them referring to a file transfer. Clinton apparently did both, but since the e-mails given to the FBI were on a flash-drive, the term dump really did not fit the scenario.

Podesta's e-mails showed the interaction between the Clinton Foundation, Teneo, Hillary's campaign and the State Department. It showed a clear pattern of powerful people paying for access to politicians.

Podesta was the person who suggested that the campaign should deflect attention by suggesting Trump had connections to the Russians. It was Podesta who had substantial monetary connections to Russia. John Podesta sat on the board of a small energy company alongside Russian officials that received $35 million from a Putin-connected Russian government fund.

Podesta's e-mails exposed far more than this chapter or book could convey. Two more important revelations are important though. The question of whether to accept foreign donations was discussed with Mook quickly saying, "take the money" and Clinton and Abedin expressing a desire to "weigh in" on the decision. The e-mails also showed that Donna Brazile had a strong bias towards helping Hillary Clinton win, even though she was brought in as DNC chair to counter Wasserman Schultz's identical bias.

Donna Brazile:

Donna Brazile was a correspondent for the Cable News Network (CNN). She took a leave of absence to become chair of the DNC, replacing Wasserman Schultz. Her assignment with the DNC was meant as a response to the Sander's campaign that protested the bias of Wasserman Schultz and threatened to divide the democratic party. As already noted Brazile also had a strong bias towards helping Clinton.

Brazile took her bias to a whole new level. She accessed questions for a debate between Clinton and Sanders and provided the questions to Clinton ahead of the debate. She did the same later in a debate between Clinton and Trump. CNN claimed it did not provide Brazile with the questions and did not know how she got them.

Having questions to a debate ahead of your opponent is a clear advantage. The responses can be smoothly written, intermixed with memorable sound bites and body language can be adjusted to convey sincerity. It is far more difficult to think on your feet and provide clear responses to previously unknown questions.

In her debate against Sander's polls showed a clear victory for Sanders. CNN declared the debate a tie.

Regarding the first Clinton/Trump debate, CNN reported on September 27, 2016 that, *"By all traditional standards of debate, Mrs. Clinton crushed. She carefully marshaled her arguments and facts and then sent them into battle with a smile."*

She was prepared because she had the questions ahead of time. She had time to practice her faux smile and come across as sincere. This debate would be the only presidential debate victory for Clinton. Trump skewered Clinton in the next debates because the playing field was level.

Donna Brazile knew, or reasonably could have been expected to know that her actions were unethical. CNN knew this was a breach of ethics and distanced themselves from Brazile by terminating her employ.

The more important question involves Hillary Clinton's actions and lack of actions. Clinton knew it was unfair for her to have the questions ahead of time. If she were honest she would have made it known that the questions had been leaked to her, even if only through back channels thus providing CNN an opportunity to fix the problem by creating new questions. Hillary stayed silent and used the knowledge to her advantage. She did not expect to get caught. Ethics were not a concern for Hillary Clinton, winning was.

Tim Kaine:

Podesta provided Clinton with a list of 39 potential running mates which he divided into "food" categories; Blacks, Hispanics, Women, Whites, and in a category by himself Bernie Sanders. Clinton was to choose the Vice-Presidential candidate depending on which constituency she needed to firm up before the election. Apparently, she felt she needed to shore up the really creepy constituents because she chose Tim Kaine.

Voters had only one opportunity to see the Vice-Presidential candidates debate. The differences between

Pence and Kaine could not be more apparent. Pence was patient, composed, humble and professional.

Kaine was a train wreck. Kaine looked sloppy, was loud, rude, and aggressive. He was a freak show that at best came off as creepy and at worst came across as a mentally ill addict.

It is difficult to understand why Clinton chose Kaine as a running mate or why he ever made the list of 39 presented to her. He very likely caused more than a handful of undecided voters to vote independent.

Virginia has very liberal laws governing gifts to public officials. Kaine reported more than $160,000 in gifts from 2001 to 2009, mostly for travel to and from political events and conferences, according to disclosures compiled by the Virginia Public Access Project. The givers included political supporters, a drug company that soon after bought a facility in Virginia, and Dominion, the state's biggest provider of electricity. While this was legal under Virginia law given the allegations against the Clinton's and their foundation the choice of Kaine reinforced the notion of cronyism and pay for play politics.

Kaine is also known for being a democrat claiming that all politicians should resign over sex scandals, including Bill Clinton. Given the negative press about Bill Clinton's indiscretions during the election, it is surprising that Kaine would even be considered as Hillary's running mate.

The Washington Post on July 13, 2016 summed up Kaine's value to the Clinton campaign.

"If you want to inspire Sanders voters, he's a zero,"
said Robert Borosage, co-director of the Campaign
for America's Future, a Washington-based
progressive advocacy group. "If you want to ensure
that the African American vote turns out, he's a zero.
If you want to make a boring, safe choice, you can
choose him, but he's not going to turn out anyone to
vote."

What Happened: Corruption

Barbie wears Armani

Hillary Clinton has a well-known likeability problem. People find her to be brash, elitist, out of touch, cold, calculating and focused on self-interest. These perceptions, whether true or not, have followed her throughout her adult life. During the 2016 campaign she made several awkward attempts to connect with the common folks. The results were hilarious.

The Clinton's are wealthy by most people's standards. They are of course not as wealthy as the Trump's who earned their money collectively through the ownership of many successful companies and a few less than successful enterprises. The Clinton's still injected themselves into the life of high society. Chelsea Clinton traveled in the same society circles as Ivanka Trump. Bill and Hillary Clinton attended Donald and Melania Trump's wedding. The Clinton's had greater difficulty explaining how they earned their money though. Hillary had great difficulty connecting to the common people and by many reports loathed interacting with those not in her social circle.

On June 9, 2014, CNN commented on the disconnect. *"The Clintons left the White House more than a dozen years ago "dead broke" and in debt, according to Hillary Clinton, who defended the hefty speaking fees she commands since stepping down as secretary of state last year.*

The Clintons departed the White House in debt due to enormous legal fees. By the end of 2000, their debt *totaled somewhere between $2.28 million to $10.6 million.*

Bill Clinton made more than $9.2 million in speaking fees in 2001 and more than $9.5 million in 2002. They paid off their legal fees by 2004."

She did not mention the cause of the debt was legal fees related to the many scandals to which they were linked. She did not mention or explain how they were able to purchase 2 homes at a cost of 4.5 million dollars while in debt. She claimed the money was earned through speech fees. Her fees for one speech was 5 times the average yearly income for Americans and her husband's speeches were close to 20 times as much.

The Clinton's were never at any risk of becoming homeless or going without a meal. Her poor little rich girl scenarios being portrayed as comparable to challenges facing Americans reveal someone who is extremely out of touch with financial reality.

She needed to shed the image that she was not able to relate to the common people. She needed to be perceived as approachable and likable. The plan was to take a road trip to Iowa, stopping to meet the common folks along the way. This was meant to appear as a spontaneous interaction with the public. It was of course, scripted and staged from start to finish.

Her "Scooby" van tour was meant to convey a sense of her being an ordinary person on an extraordinary journey. The trip itself was nothing more than a sideshow with each stop carefully scripted but it was different than her approach in 2008.

According to Fox News April 13, 2015, *"In 2008, Clinton tried to create terror in her rivals by choppering in for big rallies, which reinforced what people already knew about her: She's rich, she's powerful and she plays to win. Always. This time, she's going for an aura of humility and "putting you first." She's very much following the Madison Avenue playbook of the moment."*

Even her impromptu stops for food and coffee were not left to chance. She was expected to stop at these locations and those allowed to be inside were hand chosen and vetted supporters.

According to the Daily Mail April 15, 2015, *"Her Tuesday morning visit to a coffee shop in LeClaire, Iowa was staged from beginning to end, according to Austin Bird, one of the men pictured sitting at the table with Mrs. Clinton.*

Bird told Daily Mail Online that campaign staffer Troy Price called and asked him and two other young people to meet him Tuesday morning at a restaurant in Davenport, a nearby city.

Price then drove them to the coffee house to meet Clinton after vetting them for about a half-hour.

The three got the lion's share of Mrs. Clinton's time and participated in what breathless news reports described as a 'roundtable'– the first of many in her brief Iowa campaign swing.

Bird himself is a frequent participant in Iowa Democratic Party events. He interned with President Obama's 2012 presidential re-election campaign, and was tapped to chauffeur Vice President Joe Biden in October 2014 when he visited Davenport.

'What happened is, we were just asked to be there by Troy,' Bird said Wednesday in a phone interview "

Clinton reportedly ordered a spicy masala chai tea. This may not have been the best choice of beverage if she wanted to blend in as one of the common people of Iowa.

Clinton's first official stop was at Kirkwood College. Her visit took place in an automotive workshop within the school. There were a few cars and engines set up as props but the garage lacked the one thing that all working garages have, fumes. The air was clear as can be. Clinton allowed a very small press presence in the garage and the few students who were present were hand chosen and vetted.

According to the Daily Caller, April 14, 2015, *"Hillary Clinton's effort to meet with some ordinary Iowa college students during her van tour have apparently inconvenienced those unlucky enough to be caught in her path, according to the Independent Journal Review.*

Clinton's campaign touted her visit to Kirkwood Community College in Cedar Rapids as an opportunity to discuss education policy and college affordability on the campaign trail.

However, while a few select students were meeting with Hillary, according to other students at the school, classrooms that sat along Hillary's planned walking route were put on lockdown, often leaving

*students stuck in classrooms until the presidential
candidate was no longer nearby.*

*Some students who weren't on lockdown instead
found their classes canceled entirely, because
Hillary's event took up the entire first floor of the
building it was in, even though only a few students
were directly participating.*

*Clinton's campaign has pushed her van trip across
Iowa as an effort to have "conversations with
everyday Iowans."*

Despite her team's best efforts to keep her away
from unscripted events, some managed to get past them. A
Geek Squad team offered to help her recover her lost e-
mails. Also, unscripted, Hillary had planned to drive back
with the Scooby team but instead opted for a private plane
to fly her and her companion Huma back to New York.

Scandal certainly could not elude her Scooby team
either. The van was clocked traveling at 92 miles per hour
and was also video recorded idling in a handicap parking
space. It was also learned that this was far from the
spontaneous trip Hillary portrayed it to be. She planned her
rebranding as an everyday American at the exclusive beach
estate of Oscar De La Renta. This is not the only time
Clinton failed to come across as an everyday person and
failed.

According to CNBC, June 6, 2016, *"Hillary Clinton
took a lot of flak on Monday after a report surfaced
that the presidential candidate wore a Giorgio
Armani jacket worth more than $12,000 during a
speech in April about (income) inequality.*

Clinton, who was well-known for her vast pantsuit collection, has upgraded her wardrobe during her most recent bid for president to appear more relatable." She certainly is not the only person who has worn very expensive clothes during a campaign. The problem was she was trying to shed an image of being elite and out of touch with ordinary people and the speech she was giving was on income inequality. Many on social media did not miss the irony and apparent disconnect on the part of Clinton.

The Clinton team was quick to blame the dissension on hidden sexism and pointed out that Trump often wore suits that cost 7000.00. The problem with this logic is Trump embraced his wealth, he did not hide it. Trump was somehow able to connect with the common people in a way Clinton couldn't.

> Time, July 7, 2016 summed it up nicely in stating, *"To recap, Clinton wore an Armani jacket priced at $12,495 during a speech in April in which she addressed economic issues, saying "We all know many people who are still hurting. I see it everywhere I go. The Great Recession wiped out jobs, homes, and savings, and a lot of Americans haven't yet recovered." Twitter users made their dissatisfaction known."*

Despite her attempts, Clinton could not convince anyone that she was in touch with regular Americans.

What Happened: Elitism

3 card monte DNC style

The DNC was in full protection mode trying to cover the multitude of scandals involving Hillary Clinton, her family, their foundation, her associates, and DNC staff. A variety of tactics were employed.

Clinton was encouraged by Robby Mook to use humor when discussing her e-mail scandal. The idea behind this strategy was to show that she was not worried, that there was no substance to the allegations and people should not focus on it any longer. Clinton tried the strategy.

According to the Washington Post, August 18, 2015, *"Democratic president candidate Hillary Rodham Clinton said repeatedly Tuesday that she did not know if her e-mail server, which was turned over to the FBI last week, had been wiped clean of data.*

In a testy exchange with reporters following a town hall meeting in North Las Vegas, Clinton responded, "What, like with a cloth or something?" when asked if the server had been wiped. "I don't know how it works at all," she added."

Clinton reportedly laughed at her own joke, but nobody else in the room laughed. Most people understood the gravity of placing national security at risk and probable obfuscation of documents from the public are serious breaches. It was difficult for outsiders to understand why Clinton did not seem to be taking the situation seriously.

Robby Mook then suggested that Clinton and other spokespeople try to create confusion by morphing the two major scandals (e-mail and Benghazi) into one confusing mess. When one topic was discussed, they were instructed to bring up portions of both scandals in response. The strategy played upon Americans notoriously short attention span. If things became too confusing or drawn out it was thought that most Americans would tune out, thus nullifying the impact of both scandals.

The strategy may have worked had it been employed much earlier on in the scandal investigations. Too many people were intently watching one or both investigations and the attempt to blur the two into one was noticed. Those who noticed questioned whether the democrats were confused by their own narrative or if the blurring were purposeful. We now know it was the latter.

When the DNC e-mails were compromised and made public, there was a lot of information release. Some of the information showed that the DNC rigged the primary against Bernie Sanders. Some of the information showed a willingness to accept money from foreign sources. Some showed a clear link between major foundation donors and government officials.

The DNC created a narrative that the Russians hacked the e-mails. They advanced the narrative stating that the Russians colluded with Trump to steal the e-mails. They created so much hype that people were more focused on who stole the e-mails than the highly damaging content the e-mails contained. The DNC cried foul, but obstructed any attempt by the FBI to investigate.

The Clintons and John Podesta had some nefarious connections to Russia.

According to the New York times, April 24, 2015, *"The Russian atomic energy agency, Rosatom, had taken over a Canadian company with uranium-mining stakes stretching from Central Asia to the American West. But the untold story behind that story is one that involves not just the Russian president, but also a former American president and a woman who (wanted) to be the next one.*

At the heart of the tale are several leaders of the Canadian mining industry, who have been major donors to the charitable endeavors of former President Bill Clinton and his family. Members of that group built, financed and eventually sold off to the Russians a company that would become known as Uranium One.

Beyond mines in Kazakhstan that are among the most lucrative in the world, the sale gave the Russians control of one-fifth of all uranium production capacity in the United States. Since uranium is considered a strategic asset, with implications for national security, the deal had to be approved by a committee composed of representatives from a number of United States government agencies. Among the agencies that eventually signed off was the State Department, then headed by Mr. Clinton's wife, Hillary Rodham Clinton.

As the Russians gradually assumed control of Uranium One in three separate transactions from 2009 to 2013, Canadian records show, a flow of cash made its way to the Clinton Foundation. Uranium One's chairman used his family foundation to make four donations totaling $2.35 million. Those *contributions were not publicly disclosed by the Clintons, despite an agreement Mrs. Clinton had struck with the Obama White House to publicly identify all donors. Other people with ties to the company made donations as well.*

Shortly after the Russians announced their intention to acquire a majority stake in Uranium One, Mr. Clinton received $500,000 for a Moscow speech from a Russian investment bank with links to the Kremlin that was promoting Uranium One stock.

Whether the donations played any role in the approval of the uranium deal is unknown. But the episode underscores the special ethical challenges presented by the Clinton Foundation, headed by a former president who relied heavily on foreign cash to accumulate $250 million in assets even as his wife helped steer American foreign policy as secretary of state, presiding over decisions with the potential to benefit the foundation's donors.

American political campaigns are barred from accepting foreign donations. But foreigners may give to foundations in the United States. In the days since Mrs. Clinton announced her candidacy for president, the Clinton Foundation has announced changes meant to quell longstanding concerns about potential conflicts of interest in such donations; it has limited donations from foreign governments, with many, like Russia's, barred from giving to all but its health care initiatives. That policy stops short of a more stringent agreement between Mrs. Clinton and the Obama administration that was in effect while she was secretary of state.

Either way, the Uranium One deal highlights the limits of such prohibitions. The foundation will continue to accept contributions from foreign sources whose interests, like Uranium One's, may overlap with those of foreign governments, some of which may be at odds with the United States.

Uranium investors gave millions to the Clinton Foundation while Secretary of State Hillary Rodham Clinton's office was involved in approving a Russian bid for mining assets in Kazakhstan and the United States.

The path to a Russian acquisition of American uranium deposits began in 2005 in Kazakhstan, where the Canadian mining financier Frank Giustra orchestrated his first big uranium deal, with Mr. Clinton at his side.

The two men had flown aboard Mr. Giustra's private jet to Almaty, Kazakhstan, where they dined with the authoritarian president, Nursultan A. Nazarbayev. Mr. Clinton handed the Kazakh president a propaganda coup when he expressed support for Mr. Nazarbayev's bid to head an international election monitoring group, undercutting American foreign policy and criticism of Kazakhstan's poor human rights record by, among others, his wife, then a senator.

Ian Telfer was chairman of Uranium One and made large donations to the Clinton Foundation. Mr. Giustra held a fund-raiser for the Clinton/Giustra Sustainable Growth Initiative, to which he had pledged $100 million.

*The national security issue at stake in the Uranium
One deal was not primarily about nuclear weapons
proliferation; the United States and Russia had for
years cooperated on that front, with Russia sending
enriched fuel from decommissioned warheads to be
used in American nuclear power plants in return for
raw uranium.*

*Four members of the House of Representatives
signed a letter expressing concern. Two more began
pushing legislation to kill the deal. Senator John
Barrasso, a Republican from Wyoming, where
Uranium One's largest American operation was,
wrote to President Obama, saying the deal "would
give the Russian government control over a sizable
portion of America's uranium production capacity.*

*Still, the ultimate authority to approve or reject the
Russian acquisition rested with the cabinet officials
on the foreign investment committee, including Mrs.
Clinton, whose husband was collecting millions in
donations from people associated with Uranium One.*

*Before Mrs. Clinton could assume her post as
secretary of state, the White House demanded that
she sign a memorandum of understanding placing
limits on the activities of her husband's foundation.
To avoid the perception of conflicts of interest,
beyond the ban on foreign government donations, the
foundation was required to publicly disclose all
contributors.*

*To judge from those disclosures, the only Uranium
One official to give to the Clinton Foundation was*

Mr. Telfer, and the amount was no more than $250,000.

Uranium One's Russian takeover was approved by the United States while Hillary Rodham Clinton was secretary of state.

But a review of tax records in Canada, where Mr. Telfer has a family charity called the Fernwood Foundation, shows that he donated millions of dollars more, during and after the critical time when the foreign investment committee was reviewing his deal with the Russians. With the Russians offering a special dividend, shareholders like Mr. Telfer stood to profit. The Clinton campaign left it to the foundation to reply to questions about the Fernwood donations; the foundation did not provide a response.

Mr. Telfer's undisclosed donations came in addition to between $1.3 million and $5.6 million in contributions, which were reported, from a constellation of people with ties to Uranium One. Amid this influx of Uranium One-connected money, Mr. Clinton was invited to speak in Moscow in June 2010, the same month Rosatom struck its deal for a majority stake in Uranium One.

The $500,000 fee, among Mr. Clinton's highest, was paid by Renaissance Capital, a Russian investment bank with ties to the Kremlin. Renaissance Capital would not comment on the genesis of Mr. Clinton's speech to an audience that included leading Russian officials, or on whether it was connected to the Rosatom deal.

A person with knowledge of the Clinton Foundation's fund-raising operation, who requested anonymity said that for many people, the hope is that money will in fact buy influence. Whether it actually does is another question.

Not all the committee's decisions are personally debated by the agency heads themselves; in less controversial cases, deputy or assistant secretaries may sign off. But experts and former committee members say Russia's interest in Uranium One and its American uranium reserves seemed to warrant attention at the highest levels.

Anne-Marie Slaughter, the State Department's director of policy planning at the time, said she was unaware of the transaction or the extent to which it made Russia a dominant uranium supplier. But speaking generally, she urged caution in evaluating its wisdom in hindsight.

The unease reaches beyond diplomatic circles. In Wyoming, where Uranium One equipment is scattered across his 35,000-acre ranch, John Christensen is frustrated that repeated changes in corporate ownership over the years led to French, South African, Canadian and, finally, Russian control over mining rights on his property. "I hate to see a foreign government own mining rights here in the United States," he said. "I don't think that should happen."

Regarding the DNC e-mail release it has since become known that based upon the data transfer rate, no external hacking had occurred. The data transfer rate was consistent with information being loaded to a flash drive. It was an inside job and all fingers pointed to one person, Seth Rich. Rich's murder had been designated as occurring during a botched robbery. Nothing was stolen.

Exposed e-mails from Mook and Podesta showed an ability to call upon surrogates to create mischief for the republicans.

The job of surrogates is to conduct dirty tricks that benefit one candidate without there being an obvious or direct connection to that candidate's campaign. In the 2016 campaign this took the form of paid protestors hired to disrupt and bring negative attention to opposing candidates. They are meant to appear as spontaneous anger driven protests. In this case most people responded to advertisements for "political activists" posted on such places as craigslist. It was obvious to some that these were not spontaneous protests and the protesters themselves had difficulty answering questions about why they were protesting. The truth was exposed through a series of hidden camera operations.

According to the Washington Post, October 21, 2016, *"The 16-minute video prominently features Scott Foval, of Americans United for Change and Democracy Partners, founded by Democratic political operative Robert Creamer. Both Foval and Creamer, who is married to Rep. Jan Schakowsky, lost their jobs after the video was released. In the video, Foval says he "answers to the head of special events for the DNC and the head of the special events for the campaign." Video clips from hidden cameras capture Foval describing "agitator training" and tricks used to bait Trump supporters outside rallies.*

"There's a script of engagement. Sometimes the crazies bite and sometimes the crazies don't bite," Foval says in the video, referring to Trump supporters. He said people are coached not to engage in confrontation inside rallies, because the Secret Service is in control inside. He does not specify at which or how many rallies such "conflict engagement" has taken place.

"Honestly, it's not hard to get some of these a–holes to pop off. It's a matter of showing up, to want to get into the rally, in a Planned Parenthood T-shirt. Or [say] 'Trump is a Nazi.' You know. You can message to draw them out and draw them to punch you," he says.

Foval describes his process of making sure there is a "double blind" so that the Clinton campaign and the DNC can have plausible deniability: "The thing that we have to watch is making sure there is a double blind between the actual campaign and the actual DNC and what we're doing. There's a double blind there, so they can plausibly deny that they knew anything about it."

A man who goes by both Aaron Black and Adam Minter, who describes himself as "basically deputy rapid response director for the DNC for all things Trump on the ground," takes credit for coordinating the University of Illinois at Chicago protest. "But none of this is supposed to come back to us," he says in the video. Creamer said the man was a "temporary regional subcontractor" for his firm.

"We regret the unprofessional and careless hypothetical conversations that were captured on hidden cameras of a temporary regional contractor for our firm, and he is no longer working with us. While none of the schemes described in the conversations ever took place, these conversations do not at all reflect the values of Democracy Partners," Creamer said in a statement.

DNC interim chair Donna Brazile said the practices described by the man "do not in any way comport with our long-standing policies on organizing events, and those statements and sentiments do not represent the values that the Committee holds dear."

An activist named Zulema Rodriguez says in the video that she "did the Chicago Trump event where we shut down like all the, yeah," and "then we also did the Arizona one where we shut the highway down." The Trump campaign pointed to Rodriguez as support for Trump's claim, noting that she was paid $1,610 and $30 for a phone by the Clinton campaign."

One of the DNC's most powerful surrogates is George Soros. His "charitable" activities have been banned in many countries for sedition and national security threats. He is wanted in France for a conviction of insider trading. A petition with 70,000 signatures has been presented to the U.S. government to declare Soros a terrorist based upon his funding of groups such as Antifa, Black Live Matter and other groups prone to violence. Soros donated 8 million dollars to the Hillary Clinton campaign through super PAC's.

According to the Washington Times, July 14, 2016, *"Billionaire George Soros has funded liberal organizations intent on bringing confusion, disarray and trouble to the Republican National Convention.*

Civil rights group Color of Change — which Mr. Soros gave $500,000 to in his Foundation's latest tax return — collected more than 100,000 signatures on a petition to demand Coca-Cola and other companies withdraw their support from the convention. The petition that featured a Coke bottle with the label, "Share a Coke with the KKK."

Color of Change was joined by UltraViolet, another Soros-backed women's rights organization, in the petition, an effort to amplify their collective voice against the GOP. And it worked. Coca-Cola caved to the pressure and decided to give only $75,000 to the convention, compared to the about $660,000 it gave in 2012. Other corporate sponsors were scared off.

To demonstrate how extreme Color of Change's political ideology is, it's latest campaign is to defund America's police forces that "don't defend black lives." Its social media feeds gave no reference to the five men in uniform who lost their lives in Dallas.

Brave New Films, which received $250,000 from Mr. Soros' foundation, tried to make waves for Republicans by creating misinformation about their convention through social media. Brave New Films is a social media "quick-strike capability" company that uses media, films, volunteers and internet video campaigns to "challenge mainstream media with the *truth, and motivates people to take action on social issues nationwide," according to its website.*

In a Facebook posting, Brave New Films bragged about driving a fake internet campaign, a petition to allow for open carry at the convention, into the mainstream media. The petition was reported on as if Republicans wanted it, however, it was simply created by a liberal, Soros troll. Brave New Media wrote on their Facebook page, congratulating the original scammer. "When Washington Post and other mainstream media write about your act in a serious way, you won. Respect!"

For the record: we are proud that we helped a bit, delivering over 30,000 clicks to the original petition," Brave New Media added. Deceit and lies, that's what these groups are up to, and they're using the mainstream media as their pawns.

MoveOn.org is also planning activity. They proudly took responsibility for shutting down Mr. Trump's rally in Chicago in March, and fundraised off their success. The group's been quiet about their plans for actual protests at the convention, but we can bet they'll be involved. On Wednesday MoveOn urged its members in an email to sign the "Movement for Black Lives Pledge," being circulated by Black Lives Matter activists, calling Mr. Trump a "hatemonger."

The Center for Popular Democracy (CPD), a progressive organization that was given $900,000 by Mr. Soros's Foundation, held a People's Convention in Pittsburgh, to organize social justice movements *ahead of the political conventions both in Cleveland and Philadelphia.*

The conference included Black Lives Matter organizers, those campaigning for immigration reform, the Fight for $15, LGBTQ rights, and environmental justice activists. Its purpose was to give them the tools to communicate and engage with one-another's campaigns to amplify their collective voice."

What Happened: Sedition

You've Got Mail, Somewhere

It is baffling that Hillary Clinton did not understand the risk to national security of housing a server filled with government secrets in her bathroom closet. Given her undisputed intelligence, she must have known the consequences and decided her choice was somehow worth the risk. One explanation, which she provided was convenience of using one server. A more likely reason would be that she wanted to retain control over her communications and keep them out of the public eye. Credibility is lent to the latter explanation because upon realization that she would have to turn e-mails over to the FBI, she hand-selected what would be turned over and what would be deleted.

Government computer systems are used for government business for several reasons. The first reason is security. Government agencies ensure that there is a proper level of security built into their systems to help prevent hacking attempts. Classified, secret, confidential, and top-secret information must be guarded to protect ongoing operations and human assets. As situations change, it should be anticipated that some documents will also change classification levels. Within a secure environment these changes can easily be made but within a secret and hidden private system they cannot.

Government computer systems are used to ensure that an historic record is preserved to be turned over to the national archives. These records are also meant to be made available to respond to freedom of information act requests. Revelations in the e-mail scandal are still being made daily as unknown e-mail chains are being discovered on recipient's computers that Clinton did not turn over to the

FBI. At very least, Clinton is guilty of obstructing justice by erasing 30,000 e-mails, attempting to wipe her hard drive clean, not voluntarily disclosing her use of a private server and allowing people without security clearance (her attorney) access to classified documents. At worst she jeopardized national security, destroyed official documents, and withheld information subpoenaed by congress.

Hillary Clinton's e-mail fiasco is very difficult to follow without a timeline.

The timeline excepts below, in italics, is from CNN October 28, 2016 while my comments are in standard type. *2008 -- The server used for clintonemail.com is registered under the name Eric Hoteham. This is presumably a misspelling of Eric Hothem, the name of a former Clinton aide. January 13, 2009 -- The domain clintonemail.com is registered in the name of longtime adviser to former President Bill Clinton, Justin Cooper. Hillary Clinton's email is set up as hdr22@clintonemail.com.*

Hothem and Cooper were used to create a layer of deception as to who the true owner of the site was.

2009 -- Government employees are allowed to use private emails for government work. However, this practice is strongly discouraged. If using a private email, "the agency must ensure that federal records sent or received on such systems are preserved in the appropriate agency record-keeping system."

Clinton did not preserve federal records sent or received in the appropriate agency record-keeping system. She had not, at this time, disclosed that her private server existed.

November 2012 -- Clinton's private email server was redesigned to use Google as the backup server.

Google is not immune from hacking. In early 2010 Google disclosed that there was a highly sophisticated and targeted attack on its corporate infrastructure that resulted in theft of intellectual property. It's also well known that Google collects information from all its users for its own use and in aiding law enforcement investigations. Information backed up on Google was not secure.

March 20, 2013 -- Gawker reports that based on emails retrieved by a Romanian hacker called "Guccifer," Clinton used the "clintonemail.com" domain name in emails to advisers and friends. Because her original address is revealed in the article, Clinton changes her email address.

July 2013 -- Clinton's email server is changed once again to be backed up by a McAfee-owned company.

Clinton knew that her server was vulnerable to being hacked. She still did not turn over her government e-mails for storage nor did she seek helping protect them from falling into the wrong hands.

September 2013 -- National Archives and Records Administration clarifies that personal email can only be used in "emergency situations" and that emails from personal accounts should be captured and managed in accordance with agency record-keeping practices.

Clinton's e-mail server was used for nearly all government communications and many Clinton Foundation activities. Other government officials including Huma Abedin and John Podesta used the server as well.

2014 -- The State Department requests that all former secretaries of state "submit any records in their possession for proper preservation. "Also in 2014, at the request of the State Department, Clinton hands over 55,000 pages; approximately 30,000 emails (were not turned over). Left out were emails deemed by her and her staff to be "personal."

It has since been determined by cross-referencing e-mails from recipients, that Clinton erased e-mails that were not of a personal nature. Despite her efforts to permanently wipe her hard drive, On August 30, 2017 the FBI disclosed that it recovered about half of the e-mails Clinton deemed personal and had erased. Thirty of those e-mails involved discussions about Benghazi.

December 1, 2014 -- President Barack Obama signs an update to the Federal Records Act that clarified how private emails are allowed to be used. According to the National Archives and Records Administration, this update prohibits "the use of private email accounts by government officials unless they copy or forward any such emails into their government account within 20 days."

March 3, 2015 -- Clinton spokesman Nick Merrill says: "... like secretaries of state before her, she used her own email account when engaging with any department officials." "For government business, she emailed them on their department accounts, with every expectation they would be retained. When the department asked former secretaries last year for help ensuring their emails were in fact retained, we immediately said yes." "Both the letter and spirit of the rules permitted State Department officials to use non-government email, as long as appropriate records were preserved."

Clinton tried to defer responsibility by claiming other Secretaries of State had used private e-mail for government business. Colin Powell sent 1 such e-mail and Condoleezza Rice sent of received 10. Neither had a secret private server. Most of their work was done on government computers. Provisions allow personal e-mails to be used in emergency situations, if appropriate records were preserved.

March 5, 2015 -- It is revealed that Clinton isn't publicly registered as the owner of the domain and server used to operate her personal email. This makes it more difficult to trace the account back to her. Accounts were registered in her aides' names, and she used a proxy company to shield her involvement.

March 6, 2015 -- The State Department begins reviewing emails to determine what can be publicly released, not whether Clinton did anything wrong.

March 10, 2015 -- Clinton holds a 20-minute "press encounter" at the United Nations, saying:

"I opted for convenience to use my personal email account, which was allowed by the State Department, because I thought it would be easier to carry just one device for my work and for my personal emails instead of two." "Looking back, it would have been better if I'd simply used a second email account and

carried a second phone, but at the time, this didn't seem like an issue."

Clinton never carried one device. She always had at least two, a Blackberry and a tablet computer. She also used at least 3 known e mail addresses.

March 12, 2015 -- State Department spokeswoman Jen Psaki tells reporters the State Department would remove any emails "deemed not to be agency records."

March 27, 2015 -- Rep. Trey Gowdy makes the statement, "Secretary Clinton unilaterally decided to wipe her server clean and permanently delete all emails from her personal server."

March 31, 2015 -- It is revealed that Clinton used both an iPad and a Blackberry for email, allegedly contradicting the statement she made on March 10 about not wanting to carry multiple devices.

April 15, 2015 -- It is discovered that Clinton ignored questions from Congress in 2012 about her email.

May 22, 2015 -- The first batch of emails, mostly Benghazi-related, are released. This release consisted of approximately 300 emails, which is around 850 pages.

The State Department tried to delay releasing the Clinton e-mails.

May 26, 2015 -- A federal judge orders the State Department to start releasing portions of the 30,000 emails starting June 30 and continuing every 30 days until January 29, 2016.

June 3, 2015 -- Newly released emails suggest that the National Archives and Record Administration had contacted the State Department about the preservation of Clinton's emails before she left office.

The e-mails were not turned over to the National Archives as required.

June 25, 2015 -- The State Department is missing all or part of 15 emails from Clinton's longtime confidant Sidney Blumenthal that were released by the House panel investigating Benghazi.

It was now apparent that Clinton did not turn over all her work-related e-mails as she continued to state she had.

July 7, 2015 -- CNN's Brianna Keilar has an exclusive interview with Clinton. In response to being asked about deleting 33,000 emails while under investigation by a House panel, Clinton says other secretaries of state had done the same thing.

Clinton's comment was a grand exaggeration of the truth and designed to deflect responsibility from herself to others.

July 24, 2015 -- The inspector general for the intelligence community informs members of Congress that some materials from Clinton's emails contain classified information. July 26, 2015 -- Clinton says she did not send classified emails from her private server while she was secretary of state.

Clinton was playing semantics. E-mails are sent THROUGH a private server not from.

"I am confident that I never sent nor received any information that was classified at the time it was sent and received," Clinton tells reporters in Winterset, Iowa. July 31, 2015 -- The State Department releases another batch of emails. This batch has been heavily reducted with sensitive information that needed to be kept from the public.

If information is not confidential there is no reason for it to be redacted.

August 11, 2015 -- Clinton agrees to turn over her private email server and a thumb-drive backup to authorities.

August 11, 2015 -- The intelligence community inspector general confirms that at least five emails have contained classified information

August 12, 2015 -- One of Clinton's lawyers confirms that the private server used to contain Clinton's emails from 2009-13 was turned over to the Justice Department. The server was previously wiped of data, but FBI officials are confident that the data from it will be able to be recovered. Law enforcement officials suspect that the examination will take months.

At this time, the server and thumb drives were in the custody of Clinton's attorney who did not have security clearance to view or have control over potentially confidential information. The FBI was indeed able to retrieve at least half of the erased e-mails, some of which were not of a personal nature.

*August 15, 2015 -- Clinton makes comments about
the scandal at the Iowa State Fair. Clinton repeats
her claim that she "never sent classified material on
my email, and I never received any that was marked
classified." She also says this is never brought up
when she holds town halls on the campaign trail.*

Clinton is again playing semantics. Some
information by its very nature is considered classified. The
head of each department decides the classification for other
material, which in this case was Clinton herself. The word
classified did not appear on the e-mails but the letter "C"
which stands for classified was. Clinton would later state
she did not know what the "C" stood for.

*August 18, 2015 -- Clinton tells reporters that
"nobody talks to me about it other than you guys" in
response to questions about her email. She states, as
she has before, that she handed over anything that
was thought to be work-related. "Under the law, that
decision is made by the official. I was the official. I
made those decisions," Clinton says.*

In this statement Clinton appears to be saying she
made the decision as to which e-mails to keep and which to
dispose. Her story will change several times to state her
associates or her lawyer made the decisions. She also
neglected to state that at the time she made the e-mail
deletions she was not an official anything. She was a
private citizen.

*September 9, 2015 -- During an interview on ABC
News' "World News Tonight with David Muir,"
Clinton says she should have used separate emails
for her work and her personal business, and she*

92

*apologizes for her use of a private email server. She
says, "I take responsibility, and I am trying to be as
transparent as I possibly can."*

She was not trying to be transparent, she was trying
to appear transparent. Her actions proved to be just the
opposite.

*September 25, 2015 -- An email chain between
Clinton and David Petraeus from January and
February 2009 is discovered. This causes speculation
about whether some emails on Clinton's server were
mistakenly considered personal. The emails did not
contain classified information*

*September 27, 2015 -- In an interview with "Meet the
Press," Clinton states that she did not participate in
her attorneys' review of her private server to
determine which emails needed to be handed over to
the State Department.*

Clinton had already used the defense on August 18,
2015 that she was the official and that she was the one who
made the decision what was to be kept and what was
personal. If her attorney did look at and make these
decisions she mishandled confidential information by
giving access to someone who did not have security
clearance to view it.

*September 30, 2015 -- The State Department releases
the latest batch of Clinton's emails. This batch
contains 3,849 documents from mostly 2010 and
2011. There are 215 documents that have been
retroactively upgraded to "classified" and were not
made publicly available. The new emails also show*

that there was worry about the use of private email inviting hackers.

Clinton's server was indeed attacked multiple times in November 2010 according to Bryan Pagliano, the Clinton assistant responsible for setting up her server in New York. The FBI said it discovered some hack attempts but could not say if the attempts succeeded. Clinton's server was outdated and the hacking ability of foreign hackers was too good to be able to trace them after the fact.

November 30, 2015 -- The latest and largest batch of Clinton's emails is released. This release contains more than 5,000 emails, and approximately 328 of those were retroactively classified. Also included with the emails is a chain at the center of Republican criticism of Clinton's handling of the 2012 attack on the US Consulate in Benghazi, Libya.

January 14, 2016 -- In a letter to congressional intelligence committees, Intelligence Community Inspector General I. Charles McCullough III writes that emails on Clinton's private server have been flagged for classified information, some of which is considered the highest "top secret" level of classification.

January 25, 2016 -- Attorneys for VICE News and journalist Jason Leopold tell a federal judge that a delay in releasing the remaining emails would "cause grave, incurable harm" because the releases would be after the initial presidential primaries.

February 13, 2016 -- The State Department releases 551 of Hillary Clinton's emails. Of those, 84 emails were redacted and deemed classified. February 19,

2016 -- A batch of 562 emails are released ahead of the Nevada caucuses. Of those, 64 emails were upgraded to "confidential" and heavily redacted.

February 29, 2016 -- The State Department releases the final batch of Clinton's emails. In total, more than 52,000 pages of emails have been reviewed with 2,101 being retroactively classified and 22 being upgraded to top secret. One of the final unclassified emails is being withheld from the public at the request of law enforcement.

March 9, 2016 -- The Republican National Committee files two lawsuits against the State Department asking it to release the emails of all Clinton's aides during her time there. The RNC cited violations of the Freedom of Information Act in not releasing the information in a timely manner. It asks that State release them by July 1, 2016 -- before the Democratic National Convention.

April 10, 2016 -- Obama defends Clinton in an interview on "Fox News Sunday" but "guarantees" that he will not interfere with the ongoing investigation into her private email server.

May 25, 2016 -- A State Department Inspector General report says Clinton failed to follow the rules or inform key department staff regarding her use of a private email server, according to a copy of the report obtained by CNN. The report states: "At a minimum, Secretary Clinton should have surrendered all emails dealing with Department business before leaving government service and, because she did not do so, she did not comply with the Department's policies that were implemented in accordance with the Federal Records Act."

June 9, 2016 -- Judicial Watch announces that State lawyers could not track which employees were conducting business on the Clinton email server. When asked in a court interrogatory about who used clintonemail.com addresses, the State Department lawyers objected. "State objects to this interrogatory on the grounds that it never possessed or controlled clintonemail.com, does not now possess or control clintonemail.com, and thus has no method of identifying which State Department officials and employees had and/or used an account on clintonemail.com to conduct official government business."

The suggestion by the State Department was unable to identify State Department officials and employees conducted official business using accounts on clintonemail.com sound reasonable at first impression. It is terrifying though, since official actions could have been occurring outside of the publics ability to know. All actions on Clinton's server would be kept secret and without consequence. The government computers might paint a different picture to the public than what was actually occurring, in other words there was a high potential for a shadow government situation to occur.

June 21, 2016 -- Clinton's personal email set-up caused extensive troubles inside the State Department, including her own messages to top staffers getting lost in spam filters, according to a new deposition from Abedin.

July 5, 2016 -- FBI Director James Comey states that he would not recommend charges against Clinton for her use of a private email server during her time as secretary of state. However, Comey does note that Clinton and her aides were "extremely careless" handling classified information.

Comey said much more in his statement.

According to the Washington Post July 5, 2016, *He said, "seven e-mail chains concern matters that were classified at the Top Secret/Special Access Program level when they were sent and received. These chains involved Secretary Clinton both sending e-mails about those matters and receiving e-mails from others about the same matters. There is evidence to support a conclusion that any reasonable person in Secretary Clinton's position, or in the position of those government employees with whom she was corresponding about these matters, should have known that an unclassified system was no place for that conversation."*

The same day, House Speaker Paul Ryan asks Director of National Intelligence James Clapper to deny Clinton access to any classified information for the rest of the 2016 campaign.

July 31, 2016 -- Clinton defends her use of a private email server in an interview on "Fox News Sunday." Clinton states: "[FBI Director James Comey] said my answers were truthful, and what I've said is consistent with what I have told the American people, that there were decisions discussed and made to classify retroactively certain of the emails." The

Washington Post Fact Checkers give her their lowest rating, four Pinocchios, for this statement.

Comey said no such thing. Clinton was not truthful during any part of the investigation or after.

August 9, 2016 -- Judicial Watch releases 296 pages of Clinton's emails, including 44 that Judicial Watch says were not previously handed over to the State Department. The emails raise questions about the connection between the Clinton Foundation and the State Department during her time as secretary of state.

August 18, 2016 -- A New York Times report reveals that Clinton told the FBI that Colin Powell recommended that she use a private email server during her tenure as secretary of state.

August 20, 2016 -- Powell responds to the allegations that he gave Clinton the idea to use a private email account. Powell says, "Her people are trying to pin it on me."

October 28, 2016 -- In a letter to Congress, Comey says the FBI is reviewing new emails related to Clinton's time as secretary of state, according to a letter sent to eight congressional committee chairmen. The emails are discovered as part of an investigation into Anthony Weiner and were sent or received by Clinton aide Abedin.

November 6, 2016 -- Based on a review of the newly discovered emails, Comey tells lawmakers that the agency has not changed its opinion that Clinton should not face criminal charges.

The whole story about Clinton's e-mail server may never be known. New revelations are still becoming apparent. More information about the interaction between, Obama, Bill Clinton, Loretta Lynch, and Comey are still being examined for improper influence.

Clinton did her best to present her e-mail scandal as a nothing burger but the ramifications of her actions are too great to ignore and any member of the military would be facing jail time for far less than what she is known to have done.

What Happened: Above the Law

Breaking the glass mirror

Many anticipated Hillary Clinton to be the first woman to become President of the United States. The polls suggested she was going to win by a landslide. The biased media projected the same. Despite her flaws, she was a credible candidate in many ways. Newsweek even printed 125,000 copies of their now infamous "Madam President" edition before the election began.

It is understandable that everyone including Clinton were in a state of shock when she lost. Reportedly, Cher walked into the campaign Headquarters to join the celebration, looked at the tally board and immediately walked out.

People inside the auditorium were crying openly. They awaited their candidate to come and comfort them. They were instead greeted by her campaign manager, John Podesta who told them they should go home and sleep. He also stated the election was not over. It was.

The purpose of a concession speech is to comfort and thank your supporters and to start to build unity for the nation. Clinton broke with the tradition of conceding directly after the election loss. She is now saying she was too distraught to speak that night. She probably was.

Her bubble had popped and her ceremonial glass ceiling remained. Instead of looking in the mirror and reflecting on how she ended up in this position, she looked for others to blame for her loss.

She blamed Barrack Obama for not making a forceful speech early in the election warning voters that democracy was under attack.

She blamed Bernie Sanders for resorting to innuendo and impugning her character making it difficult to reunite the party after the primaries. Sanders was much gentler than he could have been and the questions of her character were already on many people's minds.

She blamed Joe Biden for his criticism that she did not forcefully reiterate the democratic party goal to fortify the middle class. His advice was correct but she took it as criticism.

She blamed the media in general and the New York Times specifically for their unending coverage of her e-mail scandal. The media did not create the scandal and Hillary Clinton was the person who made the decision to use a personal server and obstruct access to her e-mails. This was a legitimate story of interest to many.

She blames James Comey for changing her image from that of a seasoned leader to a scandal plagued one. Scandals, however have plagued Hillary Clinton for most of her life. Comey actually did her a favor by not being more forceful in seeking prosecution.

She blamed sexism for making it tougher on her to be accepted. She never realized that the one thing she had going for her was that she is a woman. Many of her supporters championed her simply because of her gender. It was not a hindrance.

She blamed gullible Americans for voting for Trump. She did not believe Trump had plans and policies in place the way she did. Trump supporters would disagree, he had plans in place that were contrary to the democrat's desires.

She blamed Vladimir Putin for running a vendetta against her and clung to her now disproven claims that he perpetrated a covert attack on our democracy.

Bill Clinton, on the other hand, Blamed Mook and Podesta for not listening to him about the need to reach out to working class voters. He did not think Hillary nor her advisors realized how badly the economy was hurting the working class. Bill Clinton also blames the two for keeping him away from the campaign he thought he could help.

In the end, Hillary needed to look in the mirror and realize that her loss was at least in part due to her current and past actions. She now admits she made some mistakes.

In the end, Clinton was just the wrong candidate for the times.

According to the Hill, October 18, 2012, *Mrs. Clinton elaborated on her position. Secretary of State Hillary Clinton hopes to be "cheering" for the country's first female president, but said it absolutely will not be her.*

She was right.

What Happened: Blame Game

My Own Biases

Everyone has some bias including myself. In writing this book I made sure to include sources from both traditionally conservative media and traditionally liberal media. You will find citations for CNN, New York Times as well as Fox News. I believe many of these organizations produce nothing but fake news today, but there was a time when they could be respected. If I found too much bias in a report, I did not include that article in the book.

I am registered as an Independent voter. My voting record leans towards conservative candidates on the national scene. On the local scene, I am more balanced in my voting since I often can meet the candidates and recognize the impact they have had on the community.

I do not like Hillary Clinton mainly due to the concerns outlined in this book. This does not mean I hate women or democrats, my dislike is specific to her and some of her surrogates.

I certainly believe a woman can be president. Just not Hillary Clinton. I had great hope that Condoleezza Rice would join the race. I am also impressed with Nikki Haley's record and current work at the United Nations. On the left, I think Caroline Kennedy is their best hope.

I also do not hate all democrats. I was surprised during this election as to just how many of my long-term friends were liberal. We simply never talked politics. They are good people, I just don't share their political opinions.

I believe that whoever holds the office of President deserves support and respect. I did not agree with everything Bill Clinton did as President, but he was chosen to make the decisions for our country. I respected and supported the office of the President. I loved listening to his speeches. He had a gift for gab and the charisma needed to spin any story into a believable narrative. I did not agree with all his actions. His policies provided the unhindered growth of China's wealth and military and his policies caused the housing market collapse.

The first time I saw Barrack Obama was in the democratic response to the State of the Union Address. After I heard his response, I said to myself, "that man will be President someday." Most of the decisions made by Obama were not decisions I agreed with. The decisions were his to make and I respected and supported the office of President. I think his policies left America far weaker than when he arrived. I believe pulling our troops out of Iraq was a mistake. I do not think the burden placed upon American workers and employers by Universal Healthcare was understood or considered. I agree with his decision to reestablish relations with Cuba.

I support Donald Trump. I believe he is trying to get things accomplished despite the unfair and dishonest press coverage. I am appalled that the paid protests have continued under the sponsorship of George Soros who should be branded a domestic terrorist. I am embarrassed for the democratic leadership and their current infantile behavior. I believe the 2018 and 2020 elections will be a bloodbath for the left.

Trumps response to Hurricane Harvey was swift and proactive. His response to Hurricane Irma is also proactive. While nobody wants war with North Korea, North Korea is threatening our country verbally while having the weapons needed to make good on those threats. The show of strength in a region that is governed by both China and Russia is bold but necessary. If it comes to war, I believe it is better it happens in Korea than risk having nuclear weapons attack our citizens

I support our President, but I am not a "Trumpeteer". My initial support was for Rand Paul. I felt Paul was the best candidate running and wished he had the funding to stay in the campaign longer.

In writing this book I included very few opinions of my own. The few times I used speculation, I made sure to identify it as such and included it only to provide clarification. This book is written based upon verifiable sources. They are arranged to make them easier to follow.

Thank you for taking the time to read this book and your support for the causes that will share in any profits earned.

Dedication

This book is dedicated to those who had connections to the Clinton's and died under mysterious circumstances during the election. To refrain from speculation, I will simply list their names and allow you to research the connections, truths and conspiracy theories related to each.

Seth Rich

Shawn Lucas

John Ashe

Scott Makufa

Klaus Eberwein

Monica Peterson

Chester Bennington

Chris Cornell

If anything happens to me, please note the following.

1. I live in a safe area with very little crime.
2. I am a minimalist and own only what I need, I am not a prime target for robbery.
3. I am generous, if someone needs or wants something I have I usually offer it to them.
4. I am not suicidal.
5. I am a safe defensive driver.
6. I rarely even take aspirin and have no addiction to drugs or alcohol.
7. If anything were to happen to me, suspect foul play.

Bibliography

Adamcyzk, Alicia. "Hillary Clinton Wears Armani, Internet Is Outraged | Money." Time. Time, 7 June 2016.

Adesnik, David. "Hillary Can't Name Her Accomplishments as Secretary of State." Forbes. Forbes Magazine, 10 June 2014.

Becker, Jo and McIntire Mike. "Cash Flowed to Clinton Foundation Amid Russian Uranium Deal." The New York Times. The New York Times, 23 Apr. 2015.

Berman, Mark. "FBI Director Comey's Full Remarks on Clinton Email Probe." The Washington Post. WP Company, 05 July 2016.

Bunker, Theodore. "Benghazi Congressional Investigation Officially Over With Final Report." Newsmax. Independent American, 9 Sept. 2016.

Callahan, Maureen. "Despite Countless Scandals, Huma Abedin Remains a Mystery." New York Post. New York Post, 07 Nov. 2016.

Chasmar, Jessica. "Hillary Clinton, as Senator, Paid Women 72 Cents on Every Dollar Paid to Men: Report." The Washington Times. The Washington Times, 23 Feb. 2015.

Chotiner, Isaac. "Hillary Clinton Was a Mediocre Secretary of State." New Republic., 09 June 2014.

Daley, Kevin. "Hillary Was a Corporate Lawyer. A Children's Advocate? Yes, But..." Stream.org.., 29 July 2016

Fishel, Justin. "Hillary Clinton's Long-Awaited Benghazi Hearing Marked by Testy Exchanges." ABC News. ABC News Network, 22 Oct. 2015.

Gearan, Anne, and Abby Phillip. "Clinton Regrets 1996 Remark on 'super-predators' after Encounter with Activist." The Washington Post. WP Company, 25 Feb. 2016.

Gergen, David. "Who Won the Debate?" CNN. Cable News Network, 27 Sept. 2016.

Goeser NIcole, Lott, John., "Hillary's Senate Accomplishment: One Bill Enacted into Law, to Name a Federal Building." National Review. National Review, 28 July 2016

Hasson, Peter. "Obama 2008: Hillary Clinton 'Will Say Anything To Get Elected'." The Daily Caller. The Daily Caller, 09 June 2016.

Heilemann Published Nov 21, 2008, John. "The Closest of Frenemies." NYMag.com. The Power Grid, 21 Nov. 2008.

Hicks, Casey. "Timeline of Hillary Clinton's Email Scandal." CNN. Cable News Network, 07 Nov. 2016.

Katyal, Editing By Sugita. "Clinton Rules out a Presidential Run through 2016." Reuters. Thomson Reuters, 05 Nov. 2010.

Kerns, Jennifer. "Hillary's Rose Law Firm Career a Sign of What Was to Come?" The Daily Signal. The Daily Signal, 12 Mar. 2015.

Lee, Michelle Ye Hee. "Trump's Claim Tying Violence at His Rallies to the Clinton Campaign." The Washington Post. WP Company, 21 Oct. 2016

Martosko, Us Political Editor For Dailymail.com In Des Moines, Iowa, David. "Campaign Staff DROVE 'ordinary' Iowans to Hillary's First Campaign Stop - including Health Care 'lobbyist in Training' Who Was an Obama Campaign Intern and Biden Chauffeur." Daily Mail Online. Associated Newspapers, 16 Apr. 2015.

Merica, Dan. "Hillary Clinton in 2001: We Were 'dead Broke' - CNNPolitics." CNN. Cable News Network, 09 June 2014.

Murdock, Deroy. "Hillary Clinton, Bane of the Secret Service." National Review. National Review, 01 Oct. 2015.

Neff, Blake. "Hillary Visits College, Puts 'Everyday Iowans' On Lockdown." The Daily Caller. The Daily Caller, 16 Apr. 2015.

Pagliery, Jose. "The Clinton Foundation's Gender Pay Gap Worried Campaign." CNNMoney. Cable News Network, 21 Oct. 2016

Pear, Robert. "Hillary Clinton's Health Role Disputed." The New York Times. The New York Times, 05 Mar. 1993.

Riddell, Kelly. "Hillary Clinton Hits Trump on Temper, but She's No Picnic, Either." The Washington Times. The Washington Times, 23 May 2016

Riddell, Kelly. "Beware the Soros Zombies." The Washington Times. The Washington Times, 14 July 2016

Rucker, James. "How Can Black People Trust Hillary Clinton After the 2008 Campaign?" The Huffington Post. TheHuffingtonPost.com, 25 Feb. 2016.

Saxena, V. "SICK: Hillary Clinton Calls Out Families of Benghazi Victims as LIARS on Live TV." Conservative Tribune., 11 Dec. 2015

Schwartzman, Paul. "What's a Nice Guy like Sen. Tim Kaine Doing in a Campaign like This?" The Washington Post. WP Company, 14 July 2016.

Seitz-Wald, Alex. "Hillary Clinton's Strengths and Anger in White House Revealed." MSNBC. NBCUniversal News Group, 26 Nov. 2014

Tardanico, Susan. "Your Inner Circle: Beware of Suck-Ups and Yes-Men." Forbes. Forbes Magazine, 08 Mar. 2012.

Wagner, John, and Rosalind S. Helderman. "Hillary Clinton Won't Say If Her Server Was Wiped." The Washington Post. WP Company, 18 Aug. 2015.

Westwood, Sarah. "Clinton Campaign Used Benghazi as Distraction from Email Scandal." Washington Examiner. Washington Examiner, 11 Oct. 2016.

Whitten, Sarah. "Hillary Clinton Wore a $12,495 Armani Jacket during a Speech about Inequality." CNBC. CNBC, 07 June 2016.

75585214R00064

Made in the USA
Lexington, KY
19 December 2017